Arguments for a theatre
Third edition

'A manifesto as systematically unsystematic as Artaud's for a Theatre of Cruelty – a comparable mixture of self-revelation, self-concealment, anger and explosive excitement. The essays, all of them, are clamorous, challenging and eloquent. Indisputably brilliant.'

Peter Thomson, University of Exeter

The author of over thirty plays, Howard Barker has long been an implacable foe of the liberal British establishment, and champion of radical theatre world-wide. His best-known plays are *The Castle, Scenes from an Execution* and *The Possibilities*. All his plays are emotionally highly charged, intellectually stimulating and have no truck with the theatrical conventions of what he terms 'the Establishment Theatre'.

These fragments, essays, thoughts and poems on the nature of theatre likewise reject the constraints of 'objective' academic theatre criticism. Rather they explore the collision (and collusion) of intellect and artistry in the creative act. This book is more than a collection of essays: it is a cultural manifesto for Barker's own 'Theatre of catastrophe'.

Arguments for a theatre
Third edition

Howard Barker

Manchester University Press
Manchester and New York

distributed exclusively in the USA by St. Martin's Press

Copyright © Howard Barker 1989, 1993, 1997
Afterword Copyright © David Ian Rabey 1993

First published 1989 by John Calder (Publishers) Ltd.

Second edition published 1993 by Manchester University Press

This edition published by Manchester University Press
Oxford Road, Manchester M13 9NR, UK
and Room 400, 175 Fifth Avenue, New York, NY 10010, USA

Distributed exclusively in the USA by
St. Martin's Press, Inc., 175 Fifth Avenue, New York,
NY 10010, USA

Distributed exclusively in Canada by
UBC Press, University of British Columbia, 6344 Memorial Road,
Vancouver, BC, Canada V6T 1Z2

British Library Cataloguing-in-Publication Data
A catalogue record for this book is available from the British Library

Library of Congress Cataloging-in-Publication Data applied for

ISBN 0 7190 5249 1 *paperback*

First published 1997

01   00   99   10   9   8   7   6   5   4   3   2

Printed in Great Britain
by Biddles Ltd, Guildford and King's Lynn

Contents

II

Preface

The pieces collected here may be construed as theory, but theory is also rage, temper, nightmare and the suicide note, never really the measured judgement of objective minds, never simply a proposition but always an offensive or defensive act, the parrying of blows, the elaboration of an annihilation. These are scarcely arguments at all, but masquerading as arguments, possibly *reveal*, as an actor reveals by so many imitations. Theory in this instance follows on practice, the trauma of performance necessitating some return to causes, instincts, purposes, to the milieu in which theatre occurs, inevitably therefore, to democracy. These essays, poems, manifestoes, take as their starting point not only the agony of artistic production but also the agony of artistic experience, the pain not only of the creator but the pain of the witnesses. It is tragedy, therefore, that is being uttered here, as one might speak a secret curse in the confines of an alien religion. Is tragedy not the last secret of the Laughing World? The repudiation of all that entertains? Is it not in effect, a threat to civility? So Plato sensed, and the same sense of horror lingers as a monotonous bass note beating beneath the utilitarian style of most criticism today. Because tragedy remains both secret and an ecstasy, the discovery of its audience and the preparation of this audience – the shape of new theatre practice – is necessarily subterranean, nearly a conspiracy. Some of the signposts, a few of the keys, I hope are littered in these fragments, flung up from intuitions, squeezed between contradictions, dug from the humus of a prose. It has been my first principle as a dramatist, and subsequently as a director of my plays, that the author does not instruct. So what may be discovered here will not be advice, or strategy, nor even the thing conventionally known as the *useful*, for these things serve new oppressions, finally. Rather it is the sound of a style that might be heard, formed of analysis and injury, unharmonious notes which taken as a whole constitute not only a demand but also a longing ...

Plays by
Howard Barker

Stripwell *and* Claw (1977)
Fair Slaughter (1978)
That Good Between Us *and* Credentials of a Sympathiser (1980)
The Love of a Good Man *and* All Bleeding (1981)
No End of Blame (1981)
The Hang of the Gaol (1982)
The Loud Boy's Life *and* Birth on a Hard Shoulder (1983)
Victory (1983)
Crimes in Hot Countries (1984)
The Power of the Dog (1985)
Scenes from an Execution *and* The Castle (1985)
A Passion in Six Days *and* Downchild (1985)
The Possibilities (1987)
The Bite of the Night (1988)
The Last Supper (1988)
Women Beware Women (1989)
The Europeans *and* Judith (1990)
Seven Lears *and* Golgo (1990)
Collected Plays, vol. 1 (1990)
Early Hours of a Reviled Man *and* A Hard Heart (1992)
Brutopia, Uncle Vanya, Ten Dilemmas in the Life of a God *and*
Ego in Arcadia (1992)
Rome, *in* Collected Plays, vol. 2 (1993)
Hated Nightfall (1995)
Minna (1995)
Collected Plays, vol. 3 (1996)
(Uncle) Vanya (1996)
The Gaoler's Ache for the Nearly Dead (1997)
A House of Correction (1997)
Wounds to the Face (1997)
He Stumbled (forthcoming)

Poetry by
Howard Barker

Don't Exaggerate (1985)
The Breath of the Crowd (1986)
Gary the Thief/Gary Upright (1987)
Lullabies for the Impatient (1988)
The Ascent of Monte Grappa (1991)
The Tortmann Diaries (1996)

Part I

Fortynine asides for a tragic theatre*

We are living the extinction of official socialism. When the opposition loses its politics, it must root in art.

The time for satire is ended. Nothing can be satirized in the authoritarian state. It is culture reduced to playing the spoons. The stockbroker laughs, and the satirist plays the spoons.

The authoritarian art form is the musical.

The accountant is the new censor. The accountant claps his hands at the full theatre. The official socialist also hankers for the full theatre. But full for what?

In an age of populism, the progressive artist is the artist who is not afraid of silence.

The baying of an audience in pursuit of unity is a sound of despair.

In a bad time laughter is a rattle of fear.

How hard it is to sit in a silent theatre.

There is silence and silence. Like the colour black, there are colours within silence.

The silence of compulsion is the greatest achievement of the actor and the dramatist.

We must overcome the urge to do things in unison. To chant together, to hum banal tunes together, is not collectivity.

A carnival is not a revolution.

After the carnival, after the removal of the masks, you are precisely who you were before. After the tragedy, you are not certain who you are.

Ideology is the outcome of pain.

Some people want to know pain. There is no truth on the cheap.

* First published in *The Guardian*, 10 February 1986.

There are more people in pursuit of knowledge than the accountants will admit.

There is always the possibility of an avalanche of truth-seekers.

Art is a problem. The man or woman who exposes himself to art exposes himself to another problem.

It is an error typical of the accountant to think there is no audience for the problem.

Some people want to grow in their souls.

But not all people. Consequently, tragedy is elitist.

Because you cannot address everybody, you may as well address the impatient.

The opposition in art has nothing but the quality of its imagination.

The only possible resistance to a culture of banality is quality.

Because they try to debase language, the voice of the actor becomes an instrument of revolt.

The actor is both the greatest resource of freedom and the subtlest instrument of repression.

If language is restored to the actor he ruptures the imaginative blockade of the culture. If he speaks banality he piles up servitude.

Tragedy liberates language from banality. It returns poetry to speech.

Tragedy is not about reconciliation. Consequently, it is the art form for our time.

Tragedy resists the trivialization of experience, which is the project of the authoritarian regime.

People will endure anything for a grain of truth.

But not all people. Therefore a tragic theatre will be elitist.

Tragedy was impossible as long as hope was confused with comfort. Suddenly tragedy is possible again.

When a child fell under a bus they called it a tragedy. On the contrary, it was an accident. We have had a drama of accidents masquerading as tragedy.

The tragedies of the 1960s were not tragedies but failures of the social services.

The theatre must start to take its audience seriously. It must stop telling them stories they can understand.

It is not to insult an audience to offer it ambiguity.

The narrative form is dying in our hands.

In tragedy, the audience is disunited. It sits alone. It suffers alone.

In the endless drizzle of false collectivity, tragedy restores pain to the individual.

You emerge from tragedy equipped against lies. After the musical, you are anyone's fool.

Tragedy offends the sensibilities. It drags the unconscious into the public place. It therefore silences the banging of the tambourine which characterizes the authoritarian and the labourist culture alike.

It dares to be beautiful. Who talks of beauty in the theatre any more? They think it is to do with the costumes.

Beauty, which is possible only in tragedy, subverts the lie of human squalor which lies at the heart of the new authoritarianism.

When society is officially philistine, the complexity of tragedy becomes a source of resistance.

Because they have bled life out of the word freedom, the word justice attains a new significance. Only tragedy makes justice its preoccupation.

Since no art form generates action, the most appropriate art for a culture on the edge of extinction is one that stimulates pain.

The issues are never too complex for expression.

It is never too late to forestall the death of Europe.

Ye gotta laugh*

1

We grew ashamed of the I in the theatre and learned to talk of the We. Rightly, because the art is collective, and because we were doing new things, rapidly making enemies.

I also wanted to belong, and found at once the actors were the allies who knew by speaking what struck and what missed better than the managers, who are careerists or idealists, or writers, who follow each other.

I sensed the authority of the spoken word but still did not grasp its range, its arc of effect in a culture frantic with images, fevered with pictures and products, visually sick.

The word was deliberately maimed, pulped into headline or spewed into naturalistic loops. Speech, as art, was spattered with a double contempt, by the left who required workers to grunt and the right, who were coming to the masses at last, levelling princesses to the suburban mode.

When the politics broke, the We was lost in the tide. The culture, nakedly cannibalistic, lent authority to despair, made a ground for archaic theologies and permitted philistinism to parade as democratic art.

The managers leapt to sham renaissance postures, wanting power, gold, and spectacle, while the fringe, which had sheltered even those whose aesthetic was not oppositional, suffered a double relapse, a miniaturist art no longer fitting the ambition of writer or actor and shrivelling again into scenes of domestic life.

2

I did not wish for a theatre of despair, but I experienced despair. I wrote as a title, *Scenes of Overcoming*, thinking I might overcome

* Commissioned for an unpublished collection of essays. The title is the refrain of the clown McGroot from *The Power of the Dog*.

myself. I wrote also, *Choices in Reaction*, thinking of the choices I might myself have.

I always knew socialism was tragedy. I had represented it as tragedy early on, in *Fair Slaughter*. I had repeatedly studied its failure. But in the breaking of the politics of the time, I needed to know what meaning socialism had for me. I risked finding it had no meaning. It was no use repeating the catechisms. It was futile to rest a theatre on given things.

I found it possible to begin the play without socialism but to find socialism within the play. So the audience had to share my not knowing, when it was accustomed to being taught. I was in any case exhausted by certainty itself.

So the audience was sometimes angered, being used to the autocracy of the author, the Brechtian absolutism. I no longer wanted to tell the audience anything but to invite their participation in a hunting down of tolerance.

Consequently, I became less satirical, and satire had been one of my foundations, a skill I brought with me to the theatre, ready-made. But to be a satirist, you must know, and I knew less and less, not as an affectation (the conventional wisdom of diminishing knowledge) but through practical work in character.

The deterioration of habitual moral and political assumptions was the sole means by which a change in form became possible. This was inevitable at a time of political collapse. But the resistance had to lie in questions of first principle, which is the theatre's special territory. For example, our participation in acts of violence.

3

I wrote epic plays which commanded long entrances. I set my theatre in landscapes, not because I secretly wished to write film, but because the Polish swamp or the Flanders plain were manifestations of consciousness, just as the castle in *The Castle* is not set but the outcome of spiritual despair, and the burned out gaol in *The Hang of the Gaol* a massive shade of frustrated longing. But the Kremlin had to be implied by two plywood steps (*The Power of the Dog*) and the castle was shouted into place. Always the actor and the designer were flogged into substitution. This poverty of resource bore another corruption, which was to make it common belief the work was somehow remote, and the audience non-existent. The idea of the stable audience is a reactionary one, a blunt weapon used against the revolutionary text. It is a notion of the people used against people, and the sing-song of the populist state. The cultural managers will demonstrate the frivolity, the absence of concentration, the impatience, the dictatorship of television habits over the minds of the audience, but never the appetite for challenge, truth or discrimination. The Public, as an invention, becomes the enemy of the artist, a solid block of immovable entertainment-seekers whose numbers and subsequent economic power forbid intelligence. I refused this as a description of the audience and the description of myself as a problematical writer. I found, in collaboration with actors and directors, the audience for the work, sometimes half-hostile, but wanting. The tension between the audience and the play became for me an aesthetic, the nature of experience. This involved challenges to common morality, common socialism, even what passes for common humanity. So the theatre became for me a ground for assessment and potential reconstruction.

4

We make a fetish now of contradiction. We make banality of the discovery that the personal and the political do not sit, that socialism has violated as many as it has liberated, that the masses oppress as well as suffer, and that the individual is both an imperialist of the soul and the entire focus of freedom. And the contradictions pile upon each other in the Populist State. We find quality to be revolutionary, discrimination subversive, unanimity a spiritual poverty and the intelligentsia flinging its wits away, clambering through the decomposing heap of video and pop stars' bones that constitutes monetarist art. The surge of the Populist State, applauded by the left in one of its basest cultural spasms, medievalizes us, teaching us that literacy leads nowhere, that plague comes over the hill, from the Ukraine or Cumbria, and to fuck with strangers is to dice with death. All these contradictions we artistically rejoice in, finding it a sort of freedom, for the new man Brecht would have engineered is anathema to us, a mechanical proletarian cosmonaut, horribly unafraid. Our problem is to reach beyond contradiction, towards the ground of tragedy. If the legitimate incredulity which is our reaction to so much planned social disintegration is summed up in the refrain of Archie McGroot at the court of Joseph Stalin, 'Ye gotta laugh, no, ye gotta laugh!' (*Power of the Dog*) then the task of serious art is to describe not wickedness but collusion, not simply authority but submission.

5

I gnawed at English socialism for ten years (from *Claw*, through *A Passion in Six Days*, to *Downchild*), coming at last to History, which is where I had begun, neither official history nor documentary history, whose truth I deny, but the history of emotion, looking for a politics of the emotions. I discovered that the only things worth describing now are things that do not happen, just as the only history plays worth writing concern themselves with what did not occur. New writing began at the Royal Court with the description of things that were not seen (i.e. real life). Writing now has to engage with what is not seen (i.e. the imagination) because real life is annexed, reproduced, soporific. The political play showed what is, but the reaction to what is has been only laughter, and through laughter, acquiescence. The political play must now return the onus to the audience, to the soul. A theatre which dares to return the audience to its soul, which has been seen by the left for so long as given, material, finite, oppressed, will experience the hostility a wrecked ship feels for the gale.

6

The individual must be denied the sanctuary of class.

The form of the play must reflect not its ability to report certain truths which at times cannot be told elsewhere, which renders it news, but its distinctive quality as form, which is the living actor, who cannot be confused with real life.

Everything is possessed except the imagination. We have laboured through a theatre whose naturalism has consigned imagination to the same dustbin as fantasy.

The task of theatre is not to produce cohesion or the myth of solidarity but to return the individual to himself. Not 'We must act!' but 'Are we thus?'

It is a simple task to persuade an audience of a character's evil. The important task is to persuade the audience of its potential or actual participation in evil.

A moral theatre is not one which separates the sheep from

the goats (the exploited, the exploiter) but accuses the exploited also.

Plays are much too short. The manager likes the short play, it fits his wage bills. The writer of short plays thinks 'they will grow impatient with me!' Because truth is complex, art is also complex. It cannot be smashed to fit the timetable of trains.

One day a play will be written for which men and women will miss a day's work.

It is likely this play will itself be experienced as work.

7

I came to theatre ignorant of almost every classic text and with half a dozen matinees behind me. I came to it because I could write speech and was impatient with novels, but also because it existed and clamoured for big and little texts, lunchtimes, studios, events. But for many years I could not justify my being there at all. I could not find any but the most instinctive motives for art of any kind. 'I had to . . .' 'I needed to . . .'. So self in motion seemed sufficient cause. But there seemed something shameful in using so public a medium for a private end, so I invoked my socialism, and talked of 'opposition', thinking I helped a class, or at best, was testament. Later, I found in the study of the artist himself (*No End of Blame*, *Scenes from an Execution*) the cause that was neither wholly self nor the rattling egotism of entertainment (which I also owned, but was suspicious of). This was a sense of artistic responsibility both to order and to violation, on the one hand to the language and the literary culture which was equipment only a fool tossed away, either out of wrong opposition or false solidarity with the uneducated, and on the other, to the furtherest reaches of speculation whether of desire or dissolution. I found the greatest moments in theatre were the most ambiguous, and truth, a thing we now hardly dare invoke, came only by excellence of the performer grinding on the complexity of text, and when it worked, worked against the will.

Conversation with a dead poet*

Middleton. You are an irresponsible optimist. You have deprived the audience of its right to moral satisfaction. Admittedly you have provided a violent conclusion, but with only one murder, when I wrote five or six. I do think this is an encouragement to bad morals.

Barker. What I have done is to insist on the redemptive power of desire, opposing your view on the inherent corruptibility of all sex. Livia is a much greater character than you allowed her to be. In any case, it is simply unrealistic to inflict slaughter on all the participants in the interests of morality. It was quite obvious to me you did not believe in that yourself but were fulfilling a convention.

Middleton. I wrote for an authoritarian Christian society. Authoritarian but not philistine. The King had just authorized a translation of the Bible. You inhabit an authoritarian society, but a philistine one. James the First did not think it silly to be an intellectual. He liked universities. I understand your government is closing them down. But yes, the ending is conventional. I had the censor to think of. Yet I believe the characters got what they deserved.

Barker. What attracted me to your play when Max Stafford-Clark, Artistic Director of the Royal Court, offered it to me was its obsessive linkage between money, power and sex. I saw the Florentine rulers as a rapacious class, vulgar and not very patrician. The Duke is characterized by cupidity.

Middleton. I knew very little of Florence. But we had to situate our politics at a distance. Otherwise you could end up in prison. How

---

* Published in *The Times*, 6 February 1986 under the title 'The redemptive power of desire', on the occasion of the performance of Barker's version of *Women Beware Women*.

do they punish you now? By taking the theatres away? It is much simpler.

Barker. England in this era is a money and squalor society, also. The connections were obvious. And money in your text corrupts everyone, though it appears to be sex that does it. I think you were only half-aware of this. Bianca is obviously seduced by the duke's wealth, not his body or his mind. And yet she immediately falls in love with him, the sexuality catching up with the acquisitiveness. The psychology of this is profound. It made me wonder what Bianca's sexuality consisted in. So I made her ask those questions, too, at a moment of terrible crisis. It launched my entire version. People start to ask, what is desire? What does it make me do?

Middleton. Your misfortune is that you have no notion of sin. Look how you have vandalized the Cardinal. You effectively remove the moral spokesman from my play, and replace him with a voyeur, a voyeur notwithstanding his intellectualism.

Barker. His speeches were conventional homilies for which a modern audience could have no sympathy. We still have writers who lecture the audience. Arguably a play is a lecture, but it must come at them obliquely, they are trained in suspicion. For us the question of the private morality of princes, or bankers, is not of the first importance, though it is hard to resist exposing it. The question for us is whether we should tolerate the deforming social effects of bankerdom itself. The sin of the false god. So I made Livia see that her life, most of which is behind her, had been rendered futile by her class affiliations. I always insist people can be saved.

Middleton. And I insist they are lost, that they have nothing but their instinct for survival. Leantio is my greatest character, a type new in my time, commonplace in yours. A middleman for merchants, he puts his love of his career even before passion. While he's absent on business, he loses his wife. Then he tries to lock her up like a piece of silver. That is a man! But, when he is robbed, he knows how to take the next opportunity. Money comes with a lecherous old woman, and he's bought!

Barker. You call Livia lecherous. She conceived an appalling desire, perhaps.

Middleton. It kills, her, anyway.

Barker. The solution to so much corruption can only be mass-murder, people falling down trap-doors and so on. It is as if you threw up your hands on human beings and wished them to hell.

Middleton. That is where they are bound for. And in case you condemn me as a cynic, remember it was I who wrote Leantio's 'Canst thou forget / The dear pains my love took, how it has watched / Whole nights together in all weathers for thee . . .?'

Barker. But it cannot endure. There is always perdition at the end of it.

Middleton. As night follows day.

Barker. Contemporary reactionary ethics would make such a view-point welcome. We are reviving a medieval social theology in which human nature is deemed incurably corrupt in order to reconcile the poor with poverty, the sick with sickness, and the whole race with extermination. Now also money is violent, but the torturer is the accountant. We require a different form of tragedy in which the audience is encouraged, not by facile optimism or useless reconcilia-tion, but by the spectacle of extreme struggle and the affirmation of human creativity. Failure is unimportant, the attempt is all.

Middleton. This would explain your redemption of the low-life characters. Sordido in your version is a lout with a mission, and the Ward a study in pain. I think you are even more Christian than Shakespeare dared to be.

Barker. I did no more than lend them a status you suggested yourself.

Middleton. How?

Barker. By giving them so much wit. You could not resist giving them the gift of sarcasm. They are both wonderfully bitter at the expense of posturing women, and Sordido is the obvious ideal opponent for the Duke. I pushed the *nouveau riche* flavour of your Florence, its vulgarity and accompanying poverty, into a cultural

[27]

match for England now. Sordido is a model of modern youth, culturally embittered, a redundant genius who lives the life of the gutter. I massively extended the social range of your original by this one development.

Middleton. A final remark. How do you justify your continuing use of my title? What it means in my version is clear enough, but in yours?

Barker. In yours, a woman engineers the fall of a woman, for a man. That is the role of women in your time. In mine, a woman engineers the fall of a woman, but for her own enlightenment. But the pain is terrible. So the title finds an irony it never had in your play.

Middleton. May I congratulate you on assembling such a distinguished company of actors to perform this monstrous assault on the canon of English literature? It suggests to me that now, as in my time, the more ferocious the imagination, the more loyalty it commands.

On language in drama*

I would like to discard at the beginning of this paper any argument about drama's responsibilities towards naturalism or what passes for authentic speech. The defence of obscenity on the grounds that it is prevalent in the street is not one which interests me or seems specially legitimate. I have never been interested in reported speech or the reproduction of authentic voices. Only those writers and producers who claim to reflect life-as-it-is-lived are saddled with the contradiction of deleting expletives and sexual nouns whilst claiming to address people in their own tongue.

I would prefer rather to make a few points about the dramatist's responsibility to a higher truth than mere authenticity. The drama which I practise creates its own world, it does not require validation from external sources, either of ideology or of spurious realism, which is itself an ideology. It is compellingly imaginative and without responsibility to historical or political convention. The audience is made aware of this very rapidly – within a scene or two it is invited to discard its normal assumptions about the manner in which reality is reproduced. What is signalled is the appearance of different dramatic values and what is witnessed is not the reiteration of common knowledge but a dislocation of perceptions – in other words, it is engaging with a work of art in which the normal criteria of offence and empathy are abolished. I would stress that this is nothing at all to do with entertainment, which is perfectly able to operate within a limited vocabulary for the simple reason that it operates within a limited range of emotions. A tragic drama exposes the entire range of human emotions and attempts to extend it, and it entails an obligation to explore, describe and speculate on all areas of human experience. Language is the means by which emotion is

* Given as a paper at the BBC Seminar on Obscene Language on 14 June 1988 and subsequently published in the *Independent* on 20 June 1988 under the title 'Irreplaceable words'.

[29]

conveyed – in radio almost entirely so – and the two or three words we are so often exercised about are among the most highly charged in the vocabulary. Because of the responsibility of drama to emotional truth, these words cannot simply be abolished. The bland question so often put to writers, 'Do you really need those words?' rings with a false innocence. The hidden meaning of this question is 'Do you really need those feelings?' and attempts to restrict vocabulary are invariably attempts to restrict emotion. The words are irreplaceable for the reason that they are charged with a combined fear and longing. It is not for nothing that the word 'cunt' operates both as the most extreme notation of abuse and also the furtherest reach of desire, and not only in male speech, and in attempting to eliminate the word the thing itself is eliminated, since nothing can stand in for it. Since what cannot be expressed cannot exist dramatically, the attempt to abolish the word becomes an attack on the body itself – a veiled attempt to remove the body from dramatic space. The debate about words becomes a debate about the body, who owns it, and who describes it, and if the words are forbidden to the artist, the body reverts to the doctor. I would suggest that the aim of the language censor is to return the body to the biology class where eroticism is displaced and desire corrupted into a squalid fetishism. Furthermore, I would propose that those who seek to inhibit emotion in drama through the concept of obscenity betray a contempt for the audience. The false notion of a guardianship of values is in effect a bid for moral engineering.

I am a writer who has made and still does make conscious use of words conventionally described as obscene. I use them with calculation and discrimination for their dramatic effect. I place the words in the mouths of certain characters sometimes abusively, sometimes erotically, and sometimes with calculated excess, and always with the deliberate intention of creating the unease in the audience which is for me the condition of experiencing tragedy, an unease which is at the opposite pole from the apathy an audience feels in a state of entertainment. Drama, as I suggested above, is not life described but life imagined, it is possibility and not reproduction. The idea of obscenity is related to shame, and shame can be both employed and overcome by the fullest commitment of the actor and writer to the emotion described, to its validity and truth, and where this occurs the initial frisson of discomfort experienced by the audience in the presence of an actor arguing the body is replaced by an awe for the powers of human emotion. In this way the obscenity becomes a ground for moral revaluation.

Radical elitism in the theatre*

Most theatre managements, literary departments and directors
would claim to be liberals, and class, gender, sexuality, violence,
iconoclasm and blasphemy have all been welcome on their stages.
There is only one sin left, and it is identified as elitism, a sin for
which the left and right share an obsessive contempt, and consequently, it is a sin with compelling attractions. I would like to say a
few things about sinning in the contemporary theatre, about sinners
in art, and how I came to be one.

Like most fallen souls, I never meant it. I intended to be cruel,
and witty, and in the old-fashioned sense, realistic . . . So I described
what I knew, and after one short play, I had no more to add. I
achieved a promising debut, but I sensed in the vaguest way I had
not employed my imagination at all, I had merely reported on
conditions. I was never to become a Royal Court writer. To articulate
the profound dissatisfaction I felt took me a number of years. All I
had to go on was a sense of opposition. I now know that what I
wanted was a licence to speculate in a theatre that was resolutely
naturalistic, and the courage to dream in a medium which had
become reverential towards journalism and consequently, crucially
documentary. This genre, of course, had its political gestation. In
the post-war period identified around 1956, the bourgeois intellectuals
who dominated and continue to dominate the theatre located not only
the progressive, but also the sexual and the vigorous, in the working
class, but being class-constructed themselves, took an essentially
pessimistic view of the class's potentialities. Principally, they believed
it lacked imagination. They wanted to know it, but only in forms
they themselves constructed, principally, the theatrical form of
naturalism . . .

To an extent 1950s naturalism and 1960s political theatre were

* Given as a paper at University of Cork, 21 November 1987, and subsequently
published under the title 'The possibilities', *Plays and Players*, March 1988.

reactions against an effete and pseudo-poetical theatre which had surfaced after the war, a theatre whose anaemic rhythms and sham history made the thirst for an art closer to the life of 'ordinary people' more extreme. The headlong rush towards documentary theatre, which reached its apotheosis in the methods of the Joint Stock Theatre in the 1970s, sanctified research and the collective, emphasized 'relevance' as socially useful, and diminished the authorial identity. The writer remained the chief constructor of the play, but the onus was upon him to employ experience gained in collective work by the company, and the primacy of the message could not be concealed. The emphasis remained largely what it had been throughout the 1950s and 1960s – the exposure of living conditions, the exposure of capitalist rackets, the deprivation of classes. There is little ambiguity in the Royal Court play of the last 25 years, other than that surrounding the circumstances of its production.

In common with other writers I had made attempts on the naturalistic play by a number of means. Firstly, satire, secondly, in my case, by the effective banning of the room. There are rooms in my plays but they are peculiar rooms, rarely domestic and usually varieties of torture chambers . . . There are gymnasiums, banqueting halls, castles, burned-out gaols, but few domestic interiors. Unconsciously, I was resisting the reconciliation that the home enforces, for behind all domestic drama lies the spectre of reconciliation. Once the walls were taken down and the home abolished, imagination was liberated and speculation became possible. I was however, blocked from further progress by the very device which had initially released me from the naturalistic theatre: satire. The ease with which I could switch to a satirical mode is obvious from nearly any text. Tragedy, which was the only route, was effectively blocked by this recurrent impulse. A very good example of this is *The Power of the Dog*, which opens with a scene in which Churchill and Stalin divide the world, the Yalta meeting. So grotesque was the politics enacted at this moment in history that I could neither view it objectively nor discover a tragic form for it. The inescapable baseness of power broking on this scale commanded a satirical response, and it remains perhaps the finest satirical scene I have attempted, arguably dwarfing the anti-historical scenes that make up the bulk of the play . . . I would argue that it is not possible to destroy your enemies by comedy. The comedy that exists in my work is a cruel one, and the laughter that emerges uneasily from it is a laughter of disbelief and not a laugh of public unity . . . I realized that my theatre would be about dislocation and not unification. I knew the laugh I wanted would be strained and born of a profound confusion, or, as I wrote in the long poem *Don't Exaggerate* that Ian McDiarmid has so brilliantly performed, 'The irresistible collapse of words before the spectacle of unbidden truth'. I was wading into the heresy that would serve to isolate me from powerful elements in the English theatre . . .

The volume of massaging theatre produced by our major companies does not, peculiarly, indicate a lack of moral commitment. It is not a pure hunger for gold that has driven some of our best directors into the world of the musical. They may believe the conventional wisdom that art never changes anything, but in their hearts they are the tin crusaders of the new populism, with a positively renaissance appetite for personal gain on the one hand but a knocked-together ideology on the other. They think of an audience as something not to be trusted, as a semi-educated mass in need of protection, and protection in particular from complexity, ambiguity, and the potential disorder which lurks behind the imagination. With the end of full employment and the de-sanctification of welfare, the old liberal urge to please a morally confused and unhappy public by uniting it behind shallow collective responses became overwhelming. The conditions for the creation of Populist Theatre were all present when Thatcher took office. But the orchestration of populism was delegated to the liberal left who have, despite the apparently sweeping effects of political revolution, been left securely in office.

I must own up to the fact that even before I was identified as an artistic sinner conditions were never easy for my plays to find producers. I have described elsewhere the weary travels of my texts, and arguably the best ones suffered the longest. *Victory*, *The Castle*, *Crimes in Hot Countries*, *The Power of the Dog*, *The Love of a Good Man*, *Claw*, all waited years to find theatres. My major play on Helen of Troy, *The Bite of the Night*, has been abandoned by the Royal Court, who commissioned it, and has found no other home.* My play *The Europeans*, commissioned by the Royal Shakespeare Company, has been returned after a silence of nine months. The National Theatre has been offered every play of mine in the last ten years and ignored every one. And so on. I have been encouraged to join the actors Kenny Ireland and Hugh Fraser to set up a new

* Produced by the RSC at The Pit, August 1988, in a production by Danny Boyle.

company whose sole function is the production of Barker plays, The Wrestling School.*

A public has appeared for my theatre which does not appear to suffer offence in the way its guardians do, or more precisely, it is prepared to study its offence. In the midst of a surge in comedy and musical, a demand for intellectual intransigence has made itself apparent. This public appetite for the play of pain and problem made itself apparent during the season of my work at the RSC's Pit Theatre in 1985. The outstanding success of all the plays, but in particular of *The Castle*, a work of unremitting harshness conventionally described as pessimistic set in the crusades but entirely free of history, was almost certainly unexpected by the theatre management. When this season sold out, no attempt was made to extend the number of performances, nor has any plan to revive them ever been proposed . . .

It is a characteristic of this period, and one which again reminds us that nothing is what it was, and nothing will ever be what it was again, that a government of the extreme right – if that is what it is – should base its moral status on the idea of the infallibility of the People. . . . The manifestation of this inside the arts is a campaign against subsidy, and this is perfectly coherent, since if the People want your art they will obviously pay for it, and if they don't, by what right does it exist? Success here as in other fields is defined by financial return. Now this is the predictable programme of any right wing populist regime. What was unpredictable, however, was the extent of the collaboration in this exercise by proclaimed enemies of the right, who are the most vociferous in identifying the sin of elitism whether in the form of class-ownership of art forms, as in some opera, or in any art which might aspire to complexity, difficulty, or anything which has a literary tone, and I mean by that, the refusal of naturalistic speech and the elevation of language as the vehicle of complex articulation . . . It is the fate of words to pass from Heaven to Hell during the lifetime of a culture, but the degeneration of the word *elite* into an item of abuse has been more rapid than most. It stands in for anything that is not popularly and instantly comprehensible . . .

Now there is nothing at all elitist about imagination, though few are as yet entitled to exercise it for a living. This is the privilege, but

* First production *The Last Supper*, March 1988, directed by Kenny Ireland.

[35]

also the responsibility of artists. An artist uses imagination to speculate about life as it is lived, and proposes, consciously or unconsciously, life as it might be lived. The more daringly he dreams, therefore, the more subversive he becomes. I have already talked about a theatre of journalism, and a journalists' theatre certainly isn't elitist. But neither is it subversive. No journalist ever suggested the possibility of other life, he can only expose existing life, and existing life, which has become raised into a cult – and a reactionary cult – in the phenomenon of the soap opera, forbids the imaginative.

A further easy-to-identify characteristic of the elitist theatre is its relative silence. You may have noticed that we live in a laughing society. The sound of laughter, mechanically reproduced, is the sound of this era. The status of comedians has never been higher. In my latest play, *The Last Supper*, laughter has become so artificial, so mechanical, that it has ceased to be attached to human beings at all, and drifts over the landscape like a storm cloud, discharging itself over battlefields and banquets alike . . . I would suggest that a theatre which takes itself seriously – and it must do if people are to take it seriously – cannot any longer afford to be comic. In a culture of diseased comedy, it can't laugh. Secondly, in an age of obsessive information, it can't afford to be factual. Facts we have in profusion, it is judgement we require. Thirdly, it must announce that life is complicated, and things are not what they seem. And fourthly, and this is why it is a radical theatre I am proposing, it must give the audience what it cannot any longer discover anywhere else – the honour of being taken seriously.

To take an audience seriously means making demands on it of a strenuous nature. There are people who wish to be stretched, challenged, even depressed by a work of art, and who will make considerable efforts to experience those things. The notion that concentration is shrivelling to forty-second spans has gained ground in a culture of kitsch television and advertising gimmickry. Boredom is produced by a failure to stimulate the imagination, and of course, kitsch is the enemy of imagination. Where imagination is stimulated, and the emotions engaged, concentration is possible for many hours. In my own theatre, great responsibility is borne by the actor in luring the audience into the unknown life that exists in the text – and here you have a moment of the purest, most radical elitism – the actor's skill, the writer's invention, together release the mind of the observer from the blockage of unfreedom which is characterized in the feeling 'I don't know what this is about, therefore I reject it'. Instead the writer and the actor conspire to lure the mind into the unknown, the territory of possible changed perception . . . I believe in a society of increasingly restricted options that a creative mind owes it to his fellow human beings to stretch himself and them, to give others the right to be amazed, the right even to be taken to the limits of tolerance and to strain and test morality at its source.

Notes to *The Bite of the Night**

Social disfigurement finds no relief in the cosmetic of satire, which turns the object of scorn into an adored predator ('Oh, his energy, oh, his ruthlessness!').

The play for an age of fracture is itself fractured, and hard to hold, as a broken bottle is hard to hold. It is without a message. (Who trusts the message-giver any more?) But not without meaning. It is the audience who constructs the meaning. The audience experiences the play individually and not collectively. It is not led, but makes its own way through a play whose effects are cumulative. The restoration of dignity to the audience begins when the text and production accept ambiguity. If it is prepared, the audience will not struggle for permanent coherence, which is associated with the narrative of naturalism, but experience the play moment by moment, truth by truth, contradiction by contradiction. The breaking of false dramatic disciplines frees people into imagination.

Beauty, which in an era of cultivated philistinism is rare and secret, becomes a form of authentic resistance. In the theatre the restoration of beauty begins with the restoration of language.

The real end of drama in this period must be not the reproduction of reality, critical or otherwise (the traditional model of the Royal Court play, socialistic, voyeuristic), but speculation – not what is (now unbearably decadent) but what might be, what is *imaginable*. The subject then becomes not man-in-society, but knowledge itself, and the protagonist not the man-of-action (rebel or capitalist as source of pure energy) but the struggler with self. So in an era when sexuality is simultaneously cheap, domestic and soon-to-be-forbidden, desire becomes the field of inquiry most likely to stimulate a creative disorder.

The Bite of the Night is not contemporary, nor satirical, neither is

* First published as a programme note to a selective reading of the play, the Royal Court Theatre, 1987.

it short. It is mythical, tragic and very long. It is not a play of convenience, but full of demands, on tolerance and conscience. By the use of prologues and interludes it both reaffirms ancient traditions of theatre (a place of argument and ideological war within theatre itself) and ruptures the sequential, all-knowing character of most contemporary theatre. It expects no unity of response but encourages division, and restores responsibility to the audience. Thus to sense confusion is positive, and to laugh uneasily is to discover complexity, which is our greatest hope.

Prologues to *The Bite of the Night*

First prologue

They brought a woman from the street
And made her sit in the stalls
By threats
By bribes
By flattery
Obliging her to share a little of her life with actors

But I don't understand art

Sit still, they said

But I don't want to see sad things

Sit still, they said

And she listened to everything
Understanding some things
But not others
Laughing rarely, and always without knowing why
Sometimes suffering disgust
Sometimes thoroughly amazed
And in the light again said

If that's art I think it is hard work
It was beyond me
So much of it beyond my actual life

But something troubled her
Something gnawed her peace
And she came a second time, armoured with friends

Sit still, she said

And again, she listened to everything
This time understanding different things

This time untroubled that some things
Could not be understood
Laughing rarely but now without shame
Sometimes suffering disgust
Sometimes thoroughly amazed
And in the light again said

That is art, it is hard work

And one friend said, too hard for me
And the other said if you will
I will come again

Because I found it hard I felt honoured

Second prologue

It is not true that everyone wants to be
Entertained
Some want the pain of unknowing
Shh
Shh
Shh
The ecstasy of not knowing for once
The sheer suspension of not knowing
Shh
Shh
Shh
Three students in a smoke-filled room
Three girls on holiday
A pregnancy on a Saturday night
I knew that
I knew that
I already knew that

The marriage which was hardly
The socialist who wasn't
The American with the plague
I knew that
I knew that
I already knew that

We can go home now
Oh, car seat kiss my arse
We can go home now
Oh, underground upholstery
Caress my buttock
I loved that play it was so true
Take your skirt off
I loved that play it was so
Take your skirt off
What else are theatres for
Take your skirt off

This has to be the age for more musicals
Declares the manager
The people are depressed

This has to be the age for more musicals
Declares the careerist
Who thinks the tilted face is power
Who believes humming is believing

No
The problems are different
They are
They really are
I say this with all the circumspection
A brute can muster

I ask you
Hatred apart
Abuse apart
Boredom in abeyance
Politics in the cupboard
Anger in the drawer
Should we not

I know it's impossible but you still try

Not reach down beyond the known for once

I'll take you
I'll hold your throat
I will

And vomit I will tolerate
Over my shirt
Over my wrists
Your bile
Your juices
I'll be your guide
And whistler in the dark
Cougher over filthy words
And all known sentiments recycled for this house

Clarity
Meaning
Logic
And Consistency

None of it
None

I honour you too much
To paste you with what you already know so

Beyond the slums of England
Tower blocks floating on ponds of urine
Like the lighthouse on its bed of mercury

Beyond the screams of women fouled
Who have lost sight and sense of all desire

And grinning classes of male satirists
Beyond
The witty deconstruction of the literary myth
And individuals in the web of class
No ideology on the cheap
No ideology on the cheap

You think a thing repeated three times is a truth
You think to sing along is solidarity

No ideology on the cheap

Apologies
Old spasms
Apologies
Old temper

Apologies
Apologies

I charm you
Like the Viennese professor in the desert
Of America
My smile is a crack of pain
Like the exiled pianist in the tart's embrace
My worn fingers reach for your place
Efficiently

It's an obligation . . .

Honouring the audience*

Obviously, the English theatre is in crisis. Equally obviously, its crisis reflects the crisis in the liberal intelligentsia which owns the theatre. This crisis is an intellectual one. The question, 'What kind of theatre do we want?' is best answered from the point of view of 'What kind of audience do we want?' We are in fear of our own audience, as a poor teacher is afraid of the class.

The word which has seeped into the vocabulary is Celebration. We do not know what to celebrate however, if only because at certain times there is nothing to celebrate. The theatre we have created celebrates nothing, though it is usually filled with laughter. Laughter appears to be a manifestation of solidarity, but it is now more often a sign of subordination. It is pain that the audience needs to experience, and not contempt. We have a theatre of contempt masquerading as comedy.

The liberal theatre wants to give messages. It has always wanted to give messages, it is its way of handling conscience. But no one believes the messages, even while they applaud them. We are in a profound contradiction when the audience claps what it no longer honestly believes.

It is always the case that the audience is willing to know more, and to endure more, than the dramatist or producer trusts it with. The audience has been treated as a child even by the best theatres. It has been led to the meaning, as if truth were a lunch. The theatre is not a disseminator of truth but a provider of versions. Its statements are provisional. In a time when nothing is clear, the inflicting of clarity is a stale arrogance.

* First published in *City Limits*, 25 February 1988 under the title 'Honour thy audience'.

A new theatre will not be ashamed of its complexity or the absence of ideology. It will feel no obligations to lived life or to the journalistic impulse to expose conditions. It will not be about conditions at all. A theatre of conditions is a profoundly reactionary one, just as the insistently ideological is also reactionary. Like a party poster with its jabbing finger, it impels you to tear it from the wall. A new theatre will not force anyone to be free. Rather it will be an invitation to ask what freedom is.

A new theatre will put its faith in the will to knowledge, not knowledge given by the knowing, but the individual will to knowledge which is elicited by the experience of contradiction in the theatre. The dramatist explores the terrain, half-knowing, half-ignorant. His journey is mapped by the actors. The audience participate in the struggle to make sense of the journey, which becomes their journey also. Consequently, what is achieved by them is achieved individually and not collectively. There is no official interpretation.

A theatre which honours its audience will not therefore make an icon of clarity. If a scene might mean two things it should not be reduced to one. If a speech contains its opposite it should be played for its opposites. This is not to say a new theatre will 'see both sides of the question', which is impotence and stagnation. It will rather emphasize the essential instability of character and the untrustworthiness of opinion. We need a theatre of Anti-Parable, in which the moral is made by the audience and not by the actor. Naturally, this means the parable will be interpreted differently by different individuals. A good parable should provoke an argument and not a submissive nod of the head.

A theatre which honours its audience permits them to escape the nightmare of being entertained, to be left hungry, because theatre is not the providing of lunch. Until the theatre is seen as something other than a soup kitchen for the rich or a doss-house for the angry it will not be honoured in its turn, for the tramp is never grateful to the charity, any more than the plutocrat respects a waiter.

A theatre which honours its audience will demand of its writers that they write in hazard of their consciences, for writers are paid to think dangerously, they are the explorers of the imagination, the audience expects it of them. If they think safely, what is the virtue of them? Do you want to pay £10 to be told what you knew already? That is theft. Do you want to agree all the time? That is flattery, and the audience is always flattered, which is why it has become so sleek.

An honoured audience will quarrel with what it has seen, it will go home in a state of anger, not because it disapproves, but because it has been taken where it was reluctant to go. Thus morality is created in art, by exposure to pain and the illegitimate thought.

A new theatre will concede nothing to its audience, and the new audience will demand that nothing is conceded to it. It will demand the fullest expression of complexity, it will command the problem is exposed (but not solved). This new audience will demand more of the writers and the actor, and will itself set the pace of change. Only when the audience is insisting on change can the theatre be said to be in full flood. As things stand the audience is served, and its semi-conscious applause is deemed success. But genuine success is the point at which the audience, in a state of supreme seriousness, demands to be pulled further into the problem.

A new theatre will be over-ambitious. It will not settle for anything less than a full company of actors. The stage should swarm with life. No new writer should be taught economy, no matter what the economy demands. The new writer should be shown that the stage is a relentless space and never a room. If the new writer is taught economy the theatre will itself shrink to the size of an attic. It is probably time to shut the studio theatres in the interests of the theatre.

It was once believed that the writer who wrote for himself would end up speaking to himself. It was believed the writer had to write for others, i.e. using accepted practices of listening and seeing. But only the writer who truly invents for himself will acquire the audience who hungers for his invention.

The politics beyond the politics*

In an era of authoritarian government the best theatre might learn a different function. Abandoning entertainment to the mechanical and electronic, it might engage with conscience at the deepest level. To achieve this it would learn to discard the subtle counter-authoritarianism that lurks behind all satire, and cease its unacknowledged collaboration with the ruling order by not reproducing its stereotypes. It would unburden itself of an increasingly irrelevant didacticism and evolve new relationships with its audience which were themselves essentially non-authoritarian.

How might this be achieved? A first step might be the recognition that living in a society disciplined by moral imperatives of gross simplicity, complexity itself, ambiguity itself, is a political posture of profound strength. The play which makes demands of its audience, both of an emotional and an interpretive nature, becomes a source of freedom, necessarily hard won. The play which refuses the message, the lecture, the conscience-ridden exposé, but which insists upon the inventive and imaginative at every point, creates new tensions in a blandly entertainment-led culture.

The dramatist's obligation becomes an obligation not to a political position (the obvious necessity for socialism, etc., the obvious necessity for welfare, change, for kindness, etc.) but to his own imagination. His function becomes not to educate by his superior political knowledge, for who can trust that? but to lead into moral conflict by his superior imagination. He does not tailor his thought to an ideology, but allows it to range freely over a landscape in which he himself should experience insecurity, exposing his own morality, his own politics, to damage on the way. In an age of unitary thought and propaganda, this is his first responsibility. He forsakes in doing so his right to tell, he is destabilized, and this produces a critical attitude in his audience, which, since it is so bred into the doctrine

* Unpublished essay commissioned by the *Sunday Times*, 1988.

of messages, experiences at first the alienation felt by any public confronting a new art.

All this implies a tragic theatre. It implies the possibility of pessimism, which is wrongly associated by some with political reaction. It is a long time since my own theatre attempted acts of political instruction, though its satirical qualities always contained the hidden imperatives implicit in the form. *Victory* approached the problem of life in a post-liberal era by posing a series of accommodations, none of them respectable. Its pessimism was compensated for by its imaginative daring, its rupturing of moralities. *The Castle*'s interminable struggle between warped souls was never resolved – the play precisely lacked a politics of position – but its tragic scale, and the excoriation of feeling, lent to its audience a power to find confidence in catastrophe itself. In *The Possibilities* I recouped from a series of appalling situations a will to human dignity and complexity that came precisely from the absence of conventional politics. The unpredictability of the human soul, resistant to ideology and the tortures of logic, became a source of hope, even where death was inevitable. In *The Last Supper*, the longing for authority is shown to co-exist with a longing for its obliteration, and the play's determined refusal of the message created an uneasiness which was the sign of its relevance – neither catharsis nor epic. It is the authorial voice, straining to illuminate the blind, that prevents the proper focus of meaning in a work of art. The audience itself must be encouraged to discover meaning, and in so doing, begin some form of moral reconstruction if the politics of our time is not to become yet more narrow and intellectually repetitive. The left's insistent cry for celebration and optimism in art – sinister in its populist echo of the right – implies fixed continuity in the public, whereas morality needs to be tested and re-invented by successive generations.

The dramatist's function is now a selfish one. He must expose himself to tragic possibility by dragging into the light the half-conscious, the will to power, the will to negation, the ultimate areas of imagination which the conventional political play is not equipped to deal with. When the dramatist is himself heroic in the risks he is prepared to take with his material, his audience is honoured, and through a fog of early outrage, real changes of perception become possible. Plays of information ('how wonderfully researched!'), plays of communication ('we wish you to know the following!) are outflanked by a culture now obsessively concerned with dissemination of statistics and facts which themselves do nothing to stimulate change.

The artist's response to the primacy of fact must be to revive the concept of knowledge, which is a private acquisition of an audience thinking individually and not collectively, an audience isolated in darkness and stretched to the limits of tolerance. This knowledge, because it is forbidden by moral authoritarians of both political wings, becomes the material of a new drama which regards men and women as free, cognitive, and essentially autonomous, capable of witnessing pain without the compensation of political structures.

The consolations of catastrophe*

'Once, when I saw men with miserable faces staring at the ground, I nutted them. In streets in Attica where I ran yobbish prior to the war, I said cheer up you cunt and if they did not grin to order rammed my forehead through their gristle. This was instinct but now I see it also must be politics.'

The Bite of the Night, Act I

For some years I have been attempting to create a theatre which lent its audience rights of interpretation. To do this has involved transgressing in the two sacred groves of contemporary theatre – Clarity and Realism. The text or production which is lauded for its clarity is inevitably the one which allows the least ambiguity, the least contradiction, and the least room for evading the smothering sense that someone is giving you a meaning to take away with you. It is a form of oppression masquerading as enlightenment. Similarly, the emphasis on Realism, now a term almost defunct but still plucked like the last string of a battered guitar, presupposes a moral weakness in the audience, which must be presented with positive landmarks, like posts in an estuary, if it is not to be dangerously lost in the wastes of imagination. These dominating critical categories are, however, potent only so long as there is common ethical ground among artist, actor and audience. As long as the moral landscape in which theatre operated was morally coherent, whether Christian or Bourgeois-Humanist, the artist's right to exhort, elucidate and educate was unquestioned. The last decade has indicated such a deterioration of the moral consensus that it is now reasonable to ask whether even the most cherished statements of moral rectitude command a genuine assent. For example, the voluntarist statement 'It is self-evident that all men are created equal' does not, after a decade of Thatcherism and the international retreat from Official Communism, carry the

* First published by *The Guardian*, 22 August 1988, under the title 'The triumph in defeat'.

[51]

same aura of authority that it once did. It requires examination, it requires to be reborn, and to be reborn, requires to be rediscovered. The function of a theatre in this climate, whose laissez-faire coolness among men points to further fractures in social morality in spite of all propaganda to the contrary, must be to return the responsibility for moral argument to the audience itself. I believe this offers the artist new opportunities but also demands of him new practices.

I have suggested that in certain states of society it is better to take nothing for granted, and a crisis in public morality provides an aperture for a new kind of theatre which I believe must locate its creative tension not between characters and arguments on the stage but between the audience and the stage itself. This theatre intervenes at an earlier point in human relations than that at which it has done heretofore. The usual focus of contemporary theatre is how we live with one another on given moral predicates ('it is bad to hurt people', 'the unfortunate should induce feelings of pity', etc.), but clearly there is now a problem with the predicates themselves. A braver theatre asks the audience to test the validity of the categories it believes it lives by. In other words, it is not about life as it is lived at all, but about life as it might be lived, about the thought which is not licensed, and about the abolished unconscious. Sympathy, and the sudden liquidation of sympathy, the permanent disruption of character, the instability of motive, are some of the means available to this project. The abolition of routine distinctions between good and bad actions, the sense that good and evil co-exist within the same psyche, that freedom and kindness may not be compatible, that pity is both a poison and an erotic stimulant, that laughter might be as often oppressive as it is rarely liberating, all these constitute the territory of a new theatrical practice, which lends its audience the potential of a personal re-assessment in the light of dramatic action. The consequence of this is a modern form of tragedy which I would call Catastrophism.

The fallacy most warmly embraced by the entertainment industry in times of moral uncertainty is the one which insists depressed peoples hunger for song and oblivion. But as many hunger for the problem to be embraced as hunger for its abolition. A theatre of Catastrophe, like the tragic theatre, insists on the limits of tolerance as its territory. It inhabits the area of maximum risk, both to the imagination and invention of its author, and to the comfort of its audience. It commands the loyalty and attention of those for whom the raucous repetition of social platitudes of both left and right appear as aridities. But the conflict experienced between the audience and what it witnesses, its exposure to the unbidden thought, creates pain and even resentment. It is distinctly not an experience associated with entertainment, and consequently an audience needs to be both prepared and, as is the case with all new theatre, educated in its own freedom. Not being conducted either by fetishisms of Clarity or Realism, it must be liberated from its fear of obscurity and encouraged to welcome its moments of loss. These moments of loss involve the breaking of the narrative thread, the sudden suspension of the story, the interruption of the obliquely related interlude, and a number of devices designed to complicate and to overwhelm the audience's habitual method of seeing. The panic which can seize an audience, oppressed by years of trained obeisance, at 'losing the thread' (as if life were a thread), whether the author's (who since Brecht has been given the status of a deity in modern theatre, the one who knows all and is permanently in command of his thoughts) or the director's (who must impose coherence at all costs) must be replaced by a sense of security in not knowing, and welcoming the same risks the author himself took in charting unknown territory, and the actors took in making the journey with maps. As Adorno wrote of the great nineteenth-century novels, whose ambition the theatre must imitate if it is not to be made yet more tolerable and yet more brief, it derives its meaning precisely from the dissolution of coherent meaning.

The aim of a theatre of catastrophe in overwhelming the normal barriers of tolerance in its audience opens it to the complaint most frequently levelled at my work – the charge of pessimism. But pain and apparent defeat are not synonymous with pessimism, which is a narrow concept dear to the totalitarian mind and outlawed by the totalitarian state, where the idea of 'the depressing thought' as a threat to public morale has maimed literature and art. The nauseating cheerfulness of socialist realist literature, with its exhortations and beckonings to an impossible future, forced its practitioners to exercise their depression in private and contributed to the high suicide rate among 'progressive' artists. A similar imperative to enlighten, amuse, and stimulate good thoughts of a collective nature (family, nation, party, community) clings to the carnival mania of the left and the moral crusade of the right. But the banging of the drum is hollow and the rhetoric shallow. It is simply not credible. It is not the sum of experience. The catastrophe is also the property of the people, and it is the spectacle of human pain, of charismatic defeat, that constitutes the fascination and strength of tragedy. My own theatre has never aimed for solidarity, but to address the soul where it feels its difference. It is intended to plunge beneath the ground of common belief and to test the ground of first principles. The exhaustion felt by the audience in a theatre of this nature is not enervating, but the imagination is stimulated and the structures of morality are tested, even if only to be affirmed. But it is the audience who must calibrate and assess. Traditional tragedy was a restatement of public morality over the corpse of the transgressing protagonist – thus Brecht saw catharsis as essentially passive. But in a theatre of Catastrophe there is no restoration of certitudes, and in a sense more compelling and less manipulated than in the Epic theatre, it is the audience which is freed into authority. In a culture now so rampantly populist that the cultural distinctions of right and left have evaporated, the public have a right of access to a theatre which is neither brief nor relentlessly uplifting, but which insists on complexity and pain, and the beauty that can only be created from the spectacle of pain. In Catastrophe, whose imaginative ambition exposes the reactionary content in the miserabilism of everyday life, lies the possibility of reconstruction.

Beauty and terror in the Theatre of Catastrophe*

I want to discuss the idea of beauty and its political implications in some of my plays. It seems to me there are moments of graphic beauty in the staging of certain scenes and an accompanying beauty of expression, which, despite the terror of the event described, or because of it, complicate and subvert the ostensible meaning. I believe this reflex in what might be called my writing personality accounts for the density of the experience and the impossibility of reducing it to fixed interpretations. I take it for granted, of course, that the play is not a lecture and therefore owes no duty of lucidity or total coherence.

I would like to take as a first example the final scene of an early play, *Claw*, which was first performed at Charles Marowitz's now defunct Open Space Theatre in 1975, and was my first three-act play. I regarded this play at the time as a didactic play of politics demonstrating false consciousness, the futility of individualism and the myth of social mobility. The protagonist, an illegitimate war baby, defying his stepfather's gnawing insistence on class-solidarity, succeeds brilliantly in his chosen career as a pimp. His activities place him in conflict with a government minister whom he numbers among his clients. He threatens to expose the man's private scandal, and, misjudging his own power, finds himself incarcerated in the wing of a mental hospital which is effectively a death-chamber. Alone with his two warders, one a former assistant to the now redundant hangman, the other a turned IRA man, he senses the imminence of his death and the absolute eradication of any trace of his existence. As a single individual, he faces obliteration for the arrogance of his challenge to organized authority. In his extremity, he appeals to the spirit of his stepfather, the monotonous reciter of Marxist texts, now dead or dying in a home for the aged. The ghost appears, and exhorts

* Given as a paper at the Day School on Howard Barker, Birkbeck College, London, 10 December 1988.

[55]

him to make passionate appeal to his gaolers on the ground of their common class origin, their unarticulated proletarian solidarity, and their essential frailty in a world of brute power and manipulative politics. This speech, which is at the same time a biographical adieu, sets a tone of poetry and pity which makes a painful contrast with the environment of the death cell. Now, in a supreme effort of articulation and imagination, the redeemed pimp appeals to his killers, who hear him out with a proper consideration. The pimp completes his prayer, and in a state of exhaustion, awaits their verdict. This silence is, I suggest, the supremely beautiful moment of a play which is a journey through the stagnant pool of unlived life, soiled feeling and the moral destruction of both poverty and privilege. It is also the political climax, since it proposes to the audience the possibility of celebration, redemption and revival. As in all my plays, the antipathy felt by the audience towards an unattractive protagonist has been eroded by an intimacy of feeling accumulated over a long evening – the audience wills survival on the victim. It also wills the endorsement of the political posture of the despised parent. And it finally wills the dramatic optimism usually associated with survival. But the speech fails. The warders reach for the concealed bathtub which is to be the instrument of the hero's death. He is drowned, without resistance, on the stage. Thus the optimistic possibility is exploded – if optimism it is – and didacticism is scattered in a surge of terror.

I would suggest that, despite its relative earliness as a play, this scene in *Claw* is typical of a method which characterizes my approach to the idea of political meaning. In the first place, the galloping threat of a message is annihilated by the intervention of a superior claim – that of dramatic beauty, in the same way as the potential slogan is always suffocated by the complex beauty of language delivered of its naturalistic bondage. Secondly, the visual beauty of the moment of the appeal made by the victim – his position mid-stage between two white-coated figures whose casual brutality we have at some length become acquainted with – saturates the context in which didacticism thrives. The objectification of the moment is thwarted by a complexity of emotions. Lastly, the speech itself, passionate but above all linguistically remote from common speech, even if littered with references, removes it from the realist mode. The failure of this speech, signalized not by any verbal response, but by the simple action of one of the murderers in switching on a transistor radio, is overwhelming in its horror and, assuredly, in its inevitability. In one sense, the moment confirms the worst fears of the audience, that people cannot be changed, that pity is rare, that passion is always drowned in expediency. But I would now like to suggest that the context of the scene, which is one of beauty and terror, provides a political subversion of a more complex kind than the didactic form that the play at first appeared to favour. In effect, the play subverts itself, the conclusion, in its failure to project the message, obliging the audience to digest the experience in an individual way, but the beauty of the scene forbidding its extinction in the memory. The frustration of the message sets up an anxiety, while the beauty of the scene locks it in the imagination.

Claw is an early example of what I later formulated as a drama of Catastrophe, but lacking the element of conquest which appears in the later plays. In other words, the protagonist does not reconstruct himself out of his circumstances. Claw, the name he elects for himself, is symbolic of violence, but never of discovery, and though he travels the breadth of society, he does not journey within himself.

In more recent plays, the substitution of beauty and terror for explicit political statement, the rejection of the expected line on a given subject, create those tensions in the audience that characterize the Catastrophic play. Tension is derived from the contradictory currents felt when wrong actions are passionately performed in pursuit of self-consciousness. I would like to take an example from my 1983 play, *Victory*, set during the restoration of 1660 and performed by the Joint Stock Company under Danny Boyle. The protagonist Bradshaw, widow of a republican intellectual, chooses to expose herself to the full blast of circumstances by abandoning her home, and, in gathering the dismembered parts of her husband's body, live a life of suspended morality. The act of collecting her husband together, futile as she discovers only in the final scene, is itself an act of extreme piety, but in doing so she consciously destroys in herself the moral habits of a lifetime. She creates a character better suited to the changed politics of the state. After months of criminal and vagrant existence, she arrives as a refugee in the London garden where Milton, the last representative of passionate republicanism, is being sheltered by a reactionary royalist. That is simply the first contradiction of the scene. The poet has been an intimate collaborator of Bradshaw's dead husband, and there is every reason to expect the two victims of the reactionary vendetta to throw themselves together and console themselves for disaster. But Bradshaw has banned this kind of reconciliation from her life. The spectacle of the blind Milton fills her with contempt, and in a surge of cruelty and mischief she strikes him across the face, deriding him. In this scene, which exemplifies the collapse of solidarity and the suspension of morality, the beauty of Bradshaw's exhilaration, her poetic recollection of lost and unrecoverable life, combined with her terroristic attack on a helpless man, serve to create a dramatic climate where political values are loosed into the air, and the audience, deprived of the predictable, is obliged to construct meaning for itself, at least until the stricken Milton, nursing his smacked face, settles the chaos in a moving but essentially trite revolutionary catechism.

The removal of the moral climate from a scene – or, more precisely, the suspension of moral predictability – reaches a sort of apotheosis in my work in the ten short plays called *The Possibilities*, which were seen at the Almeida in 1988 in a production by Ian McDiarmid. Each of the plays predicates a politics of oppression. In the various circumstances of the plays, historic, contemporary, theocratic or collectivist, the characters are invited to behave diplomatically, logically or expediently by superior powers. In the one play I wish to discuss here, called *Kiss My Hands*, the wife of a radical activist inadvertently betrays her husband to his murderers, who visit their home at night. She allows them entry when they plead they have a sick comrade with them. Her husband has already thoroughly rehearsed her in the rules of not opening doors, and her lapse leads to his murder. As he is dragged away to be shot, she experiences a fit of remorse and horror, and calling her child from his bedroom, she attempts to suffocate him with a pillow, staggering over the stage in a breathless struggle whose intention is to prevent the world inflicting any further damage on his innocence. Like the moment of Bradshaw's attack on Milton, this action, in its choreography and its complete surprise, is dramatically beautiful and intellectually subversive, its power deriving from what is, objectively speaking, wrong thinking. After an almost intolerable duration, the woman abandons her attempt at infanticide, recovers some degree of mental stability, and embracing her child, declares, in what must be a supreme burst of contradictory logic, that she will continue to open the door. Objectively therefore, she may be considered to be insane, since opening the door was precisely the cause of her pain. This play, like the others, offers neither advice nor instruction. It is ideologically void, and like the other two examples I have suggested, cannot be comprehended in the normal terms of political discourse. None of the three examples I have described is suggestive, nor are they manipulative of the audience in a 'realist' way, since they do not aspire to indicate 'correct' action, or 'correct' analysis. Furthermore, in their complexity and contradictory nature, they divide the audience into its individual components, a moment of fragmentation that I believe to be a significant characteristic of a theatre of Catastrophe. This return to individual pain is unassuageable through recourse to political orthodoxy, but the power of its visual and linguistic poetry enhances the nature of the problem to an extent that denies the possibility of catharsis and creates a genuine moral anxiety. In this way, catastrophic beauty is in my view more deeply subversive than critical realism purports to be.

If a theatre of Catastrophe takes as its material the individual and the individual's ability to effect self-identification in a collective or historical nightmare, the moment of beauty is the moment of collision between two wills, the will of the irrational protagonist (the non-ideological) and the will of the irrational state (the officially ideological). In my most recent play, *The Europeans*, commissioned by the RSC but deemed unsuitable for its public, the maimed casualty of a war between empires makes public her atrocity in an attempt to prevent her pain becoming subsumed in the anodyne reconciliations which pass for public history. Refusing to permit her biography to degenerate into a statistic, she delivers the child which is one of the products of her ordeal, in a public place, struggling even against the midwives to establish the primacy of her experience over the public interest. This scene, which contains all the elements which constitute beauty and terror, is deeply unsettling, but not for the obvious reason that childbirth is rarely enacted on the stage – rather, the catastrophic enterprise of the heroine at her most assertive and irrational exposes the false content of the values that are being imposed on her, and reveals pity, reconciliation and forgetfulness as instruments of political oppression, the annihilation of individual pain in collective orthodoxy. The crucial characteristic of this, as in the other examples I have given, is that the moment of beauty is also a moment of 'wrong action'. It is precisely its 'wrongness' that is the source of its disturbance. The anxiety that is experienced as a social faux pas is here enlarged into a dramatic form, but the initially offensive nature of the action is rapidly revealed to have its own justifications in the struggle of the character to achieve some self-identification: the mother wrongly trying to suffocate her child, the tramp wrongly attacking the poet, the wilful obscenity of giving birth in the gutter. The audience, forced to re-view, re-feel, a 'wrong' action, is provoked and alerted, and launched unwillingly into consideration of morality, rather than subdued by the false solidarities of critical realism.

Juha Malmivaara's *Scenes from an Execution*, Turku, Finland, 1988

Malmivaara had failed with *The Love of a Good Man*, despite the power of his production. The audience had deserted him, walking out of the theatre. When I went to receive my bouquet, I looked out into emptiness. Malmivaara needed to prove the necessity for Barker.

He made a significant discovery. He understood that with Barker the theatre itself was a barrier to communication. He recognized that the structure of the building and its status in the community were injurious to the power of the work. The theatre-as-monument infected the audience, excluding whole groups of the community and reinforcing the commoditization of art.

He chose, instead of allowing the audience to sit in judgement on the work from the jury box of the stalls, to insist on their discomfort, which was the same discomfort experienced by the actors. He made the audience pay a price for its art by placing the production in a mile-long shed. When they saw this shed, the audience knew the conditions were different. They were prepared for the play to be different, and were obliged to suspend their instincts of judgement as well as their demands for pleasure. They knew they had forfeited their rights over the actors, and instead felt privileged to witness them. It was the actors who commanded them to see, and they crowded round each other to see better, breaking the conventions of normal witnessing. It was they who made adjustments. It was they who came as innocents to the imaginative world. Malmivaara insisted they came to art in this way, disarmed.

In one scene he placed the audience in prison with the actor. In pure darkness he obliged them to experience at least one aspect of incarceration. Then, from a distance of hundreds of yards, the light of a lantern came. The relief of this light was a metaphor for hope. The audience trusted Malmivaara, whilst being uncertain what he would do with them next. This tension was the best condition for viewing the plays of Barker.

He knew the importance of difficulty in art and the repulsiveness of easy art. The difficulty of the text he counterpointed in the difficulty of the situation. But he did not fail to reward the audience. He gave them, above all, beauty. For their effort he rewarded them with things they had never seen before, just as the text insisted on things that had not been exposed before. He knew in theatre each production must give what cannot be reproduced in any other medium. So when the drunken sailors entered Galactia's studio, they careered from a vast distance, and their mayhem was a thing of beauty, in its music and its choreography. The audience knew this could never be witnessed again. They felt privileged. In an ordinary theatre they would have thought such things merely their due.

Malmivaara showed by this production the sacrifices audiences will make for art, the pain they are willing to share with the performers. He did not give them the simple gratifications of community theatre, with its known virtues and facile ends, but led them into deeper and deeper complexity by relieving them of the burden of prior knowledge, the burden of authority which is a barrier to new experience. He took control from them, and gave it to the actors. They dominated the audience, who were not raked above them like delegates.

Malmivaara understood that in the Barker play the audience must suspend its critical faculties and swallow the passing offence. It must give itself into the hands of the actors and delay its judgement while the play completes its journey. To achieve this he perfected a fluidity between scenes which overlaid each other, drawing the attention from place to place and emotion to emotion. He gave them no time to digest the experience, making the journey of the play a literal one. In this he approximated to the text itself, which is a river of words and images. In the static theatre the audience is gnawed by its lack of control. In Malmivaara's sheds the audience was propelled by the pace of the action and could not dwell on what it had experienced. The fatal inertia induced by the surroundings of the conventional theatre was therefore prohibited.

On Nigel Terry's performance of Savage, in *The Bite of the Night**

Terry welcomed the opportunity to forfeit his own glamour. He had played so many attractive men. He had been the essence of the Romantic actor. He had played Caravaggio, Charles II, Byron, King Arthur. Now he played an unhealthy fat man whose movements were essentially comic. Terry had reached a point in his life when his profoundly curious imagination led him beyond self-consciousness, and at this moment a text appeared which was a means to his growth as a performer.

Terry experienced the journey in each performance, as any good actor must. But he found in Savage the innocence which is a crucial ingredient in evil and so brought us to fresh understanding. He saw that evil was small in its origins, and begins with insignificant mischief, even in wit. He saw that it was childish. Thus he made his audience party to his ebullience. He charmed his audience with his absurdity and was not afraid of losing face, so that his cruelty came harder on the nerves, and wounded more.

He cavorted in his moments of triumph, converting his intellectual satisfactions into physical action. In that cavorting was contained the essence of evil will. By this he demonstrated the actor's choice of significant physical expression making manifest internal states. But he did not hang his performance on the hook of his gestures. He was not corrupted by his invention. He had studied the lightness of the fat man, who is neither lethargic nor clumsy, but often dances on the tips of his toes. In this lightness he reached through time to the worst of the Caesars.

He found a posture in which to watch the unforgivable act. In this posture he conveyed the combination of horror and curiosity that attends all of us in the presence of pain. Eventually, this posture developed an ease, a casualness, an objectivity, which was the essence of his corruption. In the beginning he suffered the horror of parting

* RSC Pit Theatre, 1988.

with sympathy, and at the end, he bathed in his own indifference. Thus in this figuring of the body, he revealed the labour of his journey.

Often in rehearsal he cried out 'I don't know what I'm doing!' Angrily, he contended with the most complex motivations which were not always explicit in the text. He found these by excavating himself, by going deeper into self than actors are required to go. In the risks he took with his own conscience, he enabled the audience to forgo the usual satisfactions of identification without forcing alienation upon them. He implicated them in his acts, unsettling the routine relations of actor and audience. He insisted on the humanity in inhumanity.

He controlled the language without being controlled by it. He did not allow even the moments of rhetoric to lose their thread to the character. Instead he showed the character Savage employing rhetoric as part of his own creative and imaginative world. It was not the actor Terry who became rhetorical but the character Savage indulging his rhetorical skills. But beyond this, he revealed under the performance of the rhetorician the character's will, his pain, or fear, which he demonstrated was often at variance with the content of the speech. None of this was too complex for him.

On watching a performance by life prisoners*

In the performance they affirmed the drama as freedom. They asserted the superior life of the imagination. In the moment of performance they were not in custody.

They created character from a longing for other life. They demonstrated by their conviction that drama was a necessity and not a pleasure or a diversion.

They had committed terrible acts, which made them objects of curiosity for their audience, who were not criminals. But they obliterated their reputations by their authentic portrayal of character. They shouldered away curiosity by the power of their concentration, and made the text more fascinating than their false glamour. Their concentration was greater than the concentration of professional actors, who do not bring bad reputation with them. They outplayed the voyeur.

They had no fear of the text. They were of mixed intelligence, and little education. But they showed no humility towards language or poetry. Though they had been crushed by life, and had crushed it, they responded to the power of articulation in the text which they themselves could not achieve. They felt gratitude for the existence of speech and metaphor, and made it their own, though it was not the language of the gaol. For all their appalling experience, they ached for the deeper experience of imagination.

They did not want to act what they already knew. They had no sentiment for the naturalistic mode. They wished to inhabit other life, and felt sympathy for pain in types they had never encountered, or situations they had not dreamed. In this the gaol was overcome, even while the guard dogs barked in the yard below.

In a place which licensed no pity, they found it possible to express pity. They guarded this closely, as a privilege. They shielded it from the observation of others, who would have derided it, and exposed

---

* *The Love of a Good Man*, Wormwood Scrubs, 7 July 1988, directed by Alan Cormack.

it only in the room which was called a theatre. So I learned that theatre was a place where feeling was permitted which was denied elsewhere.

They took the text to their cells and for months pored over it. In working the text they allowed the forbidden faculties to breathe, so that their performance was made both as actor but also as audience. In this they were unlike professional actors – the play was a substitute for lived life.

At the end of the performance they were locked in their cells, so the possibility of collective satisfaction was denied them. Alongside this play other prisoners performed a light comedy. These prisoners were not allowed to see the play. It was considered by the authorities that the bulk of the prisoners would object to the play. They would disrupt the production and might attack the actors. In a prison, the active power of morality, its coercive intolerance, is expressed most violently. The criminals, for all their bad acts, would not tolerate transgression. The gaol was thus a society as tightly regulated as the outside by relativist morality. In this society, microcosmically, theatre was perceived as an affront. What nourished some was abominated by others.

The offer, the reward,
and the need to disappoint

In the old theatre, the actors offered the play as a salesman displays his product – unctuously and with fake gentility. The prologue was the patter of the potentially unemployed. Thus the audience became customers, whose satisfaction was the necessary end of the performance.

In the new theatre, the audience will offer itself to the actors. It will relinquish its status as customer and abandon its expectation of reward. When it ceases to see itself as customer, it will also cease to experience offence.

The reward is a relic of the market place. The old theatre pretends to reward its audience for its effort of attendance, its effort at concentration, its surrender of futile time. You must reward the audience, say the poor critics. Why? Is theatre so intolerable? Is art not necessary for itself? The contrary is the case. It is a privilege to witness art. It is a privilege to hear good actors. In the new theatre there will be no reward because there will be no deal, no swop, or compact. The new theatre will not perceive itself as product. The audience will enter the new theatre out of necessity. In this condition, which is the compulsion of a spiritual hunger, it will cease to pass facile judgements on the play.

To escape the pernicious memory of the market place, the new theatre will dethrone its audience. The audience will no longer sit in tiers. It will not be encouraged to think itself a jury, obsessively judgemental. The actor will dominate the audience, not only by his performance, but also by his elevation above the audience. The audience is not to be rendered uncomfortable, nor attacked. We are not seeking a theatre of masochism. But it must be delivered from the shallowness of its expectations, its appetite for rewards. This narcissistic frisson is a relic of the exchange-relation, and of cultural infancy.

The infantile notion of the reward, which still dominates the serious theatre, is based on critical clichés. The audience feels the

[67]

reward if it senses the play's 'importance'. Infantile critics are forever in search of 'important' plays. The important play cannot exist, however, without denying its own importance. This is because to be recognized as such it must trade in the very cultural, political and social conventions that constitute the discourse of the world *outside* the theatre. In other words, it replaces, reorganizes, or re-perceives the elements of existent ideology. It could not avoid or demolish these without sacrificing its 'importance'. The play that fails the test of 'importance' is invariably felt to be disappointing. The Disappointing play refuses to gratify the audience's thirst for social and political repetition. It robs its audience of the grotesque satisfaction of identifying its enemies and celebrating its prior knowledge – the sickening and secret compact between the author and his audience that distinguishes liberal art.

The Disappointing play squirms away from the notion of 'importance', and instead of offering the reward, delivers the wound. The wound is the aim of the new theatre and the intention of the actor. His performance will create the wound and the wound will be the subject of continuing anxiety. Only anxiety will justify the efforts of the performance. This anxiety will come from the audience's attempt to experience the play outside the confines of ideology. Slowly, the audience will discover the new theatre to be a necessity for its moral and emotional survival. It will endure the wound as a man drawn from a swamp endures the pain of the rope.

The audience, the soul, and the stage

When did you last hear a laugh which was
Not a spasm of intoxication
Not a gesture of solidarity
Not a gurgle of vanity
The choral assent of intellectual poseurs but
The irresistible collapse of words
Before the spectacle of truth?

I never have

(*Don't Exaggerate*)

To discuss the practical or theoretical nature of a contemporary theatre it is necessary to begin from the state of public knowledge. Only from a judgement regarding the state of public knowledge, its sickness or its vitality, can the necessary forms of theatre be deduced.

The Theatre of Catastrophe takes its form from the following assessment:

That information is a universal commodity

That knowledge is forbidden

That imagination has been maimed by collectivist culture

That in this maiming the public itself has colluded

But that this collusion is nevertheless detected and is experienced as shame

The Theatre of Catastrophe addresses itself to those who suffer the maiming of the imagination. All mechanical art, all ideological art, (the entertaining, the informative) intensifies the pain but simultaneously heightens the unarticulated desire for the restitution of moral speculation, which is the business of theatre. The Theatre of Catastrophe is therefore a theatre for the offended. It has no dialogue with

Those who make poles of narrative and character

Those who proclaim clarity and responsibility

Those who ache to delight the audience

Those who think laughter is a weapon of the oppressed

Those who dream theatre tells the truth

Those who insist on the facts

Those who clamour for fantasy

Those who believe in the existence of ordinary people

The Theatre of Catastrophe is rooted in the idea of the soul, not as immortal form, not as a thing immune from damage, but as innate knowledge of other life. In some, this knowledge is nothing more than a cherished hoard of stereotypes (the sea, the sky, the prospect of love). In others, the Soul breaks with all images it senses corrupt or annexed by ideology (harmony, family, the public) and aspires to new forms. The Theatre of Catastrophe addresses those imperatives of the Soul which most writhe under reproduction. It exhilarates. It creates offence, even among the already offended. It does not limit its address to the educated, though it does not honour ignorance. Above all, it speaks a new language, which is to say it believes language to be revolutionary in a culture which degrades language and smears it as elitist. It makes language as luscious and as spiteful as love, of which it is an expression. It abhors reconciliation which is not won at terrible cost. It demands more of its audience than all existing theatre.

The audience of this theatre is in awe of the actor. It is in awe of him because the actor does not pretend to be the audience (a theatre of recognition) but asserts his difference. He both suffers more, and exposes more, than the audience anticipates. The audience of the Theatre of Catastrophe is not gratified to see its life reflected on the stage. It comes with a single desire – to witness unlived life, which the ideological and the mechanical conspire to conceal. In this, the Theatre of Catastrophe is more painful than tragedy, since tragedy consoles with restoration, the reassertion of existing moral values. The audience is not flattered with hope, but rather lent pain. It is not taught criticism, but honoured with the truth of the absence of truth. It leaves the theatre privileged, but unrewarded. It does not cluck with collective satisfaction, but divided and solitary, it labours with the burden of an art that denies assimilation.

[70]

The humanist theatre*

We all really agree.
When we laugh we are together.
Art must be understood.
Wit greases the message.
The actor is a man/woman not
unlike the author.
The production must be clear.

We celebrate our unity.
The critic is already
on our side.
The message is important.
The audience is educated
and goes home
happy
or
fortified.

The catastrophic theatre

We only sometimes agree.
Laughter conceals fear.
Art is a problem of understanding.
There is no message.
The actor is different in kind.

The audience cannot grasp
everything; nor did the author.
We quarrel to love.
The critic must suffer like
everyone else.
The play is important.
The audience is divided
and goes home
disturbed
or
amazed.

* First published in *Théâtre en Europe*, 1989.

Theatre without a conscience*

There is a type of theatre which has dominated us for the last two or three decades which takes as its starting point, its inspiration, even, the apparently selfless desire to make people better. It is the kind of theatre which begins, long before the process of writing or rehearsal, with the question, 'What do people need?' When this need has been identified, the search for a subject begins. The insatiable appetite for improving other people can be detected in the way in which writers and directors justify and advertise their efforts. If a writer is asked why he wrote a particular play he or she invariably replies 'I wanted people to understand such and such a thing better', or 'I wanted people to know how such and such a person feels', or 'I wanted to heighten their perception of such and such an issue', and even, at its most shamelessly ambitious, 'I wanted to improve the quality of people's lives.' In all these responses there is a passion to enlighten, a paternalistic beneficence, from the one who knows to the many who do not, the largesse of perception dished out in the palaver of dramatic form. This is the social hygiene of the gifted aching to illuminate the ungifted, the above-prejudice correcting the prejudiced, and the artist instructing the herd. It is the essential manner of the humanist play, which has as its project the strictly utilitarian end of making us good and happy (happiness supposed to be derived from 'understanding one another') and turning theatre into sticking plaster for the wounds of social alienation. This is the theatre of daylight, clarity and dubious truths, behind which lies the critical consensus that art is somehow to do with 'informing'. Who hasn't read again and again the satisfied reviewer announcing in these terms why he had a good night out – 'I left the theatre knowing more about this subject than when I went in . . .', 'I was enlightened about . . .', 'The play made me realize', etc., the clucking of customers who have got their fistful of knowledge, the sort of accolade that is the

* Given as a paper at the University College of Wales, Aberystwyth, 6 October 1990.

erosion of theatre as art and the triumph of a theatre of social correction. And of course, because the desire to correct and be corrected is an irrepressible human drive, the demand for such a theatre is continuous. We have had for some decades now the spectacle of dramatists who haunt the newspapers for their inspiration, indeed are wholly dependent on it, as well as theatre companies of some distinction whose most significant activity is what they call 'researching material', an activity closely related to the business of 'dramatizing' things. Theatre has no business with research, and things are not dramatized: they are either drama or they are something else. They come into existence as art, or they are not art at all, and research is something carried out by specialists called academics or non-specialists called journalists. The verb 'to dramatize' is part of the kitsch vocabulary of the theatre of issues, in which actors are employed as a means to a didactic end, the education of the ignorant audience, and by 'research' we are threatened with the spurious legitimacy of so-called facts. 'It's all right', the actors seem to tell you in researched plays, 'everything we demonstrate has occurred', is in effect 'true'. But the theatre is not true, it is not a true action, its very power, its whole authority comes from the fact that it is not true, and the idea of accuracy, or reference to a source outside the theatre walls, is fatal to its particular unsettling and revolutionary power. The moment that an action on the stage asserts its veracity by reference to known and proven action elsewhere, theatre is overwhelmed by the world, the world reclaims it. It is a symptom of the lost faith in theatre as an art form that its practitioners require the credentials of authenticity. It is the poverty of the journalist that he must provide evidence for his assertions, the frailty of the academic that he must prove and counter-prove. The theatre is without evidence, it 'makes believe', it forces belief. The audience of the theatre comes for what it cannot obtain elsewhere in any other forum. In other words, it comes for the false, it comes for the speculative and the unproven. The researched theatre says, the informative theatre says, 'we have demonstrated such and such a fact, and it will make you better to know it', a sham democracy behind which lies a repugnant arrogance. The imaginative theatre says 'we prove nothing, we assert that nothing can be proved by the actor'.

Let us not pretend, however, that the Theatre of Conscience does not have its attractions in the contemporary world. There is an

[73]

obvious base pleasure to be had in enlightenment of this kind, a gratifying trade-off between customer and performer. You pay £5 or £10 for a seat and you are sent home with an item of sympathy or knowledge, you grasp what you are intended to grasp, some facts about a researched subject, some insight into the social conditions of somebody, you are officially encouraged to extend sympathy to a chosen group of fellow human beings, which is easily done in art if not in life, and your conscience is effectively massaged. If a theatre of entertainment is a deal, so is the theatre of enlightenment. As the writer says in his interview, 'I wanted people to understand such and such a thing better', and he cannot fail as long as he contains his efforts within the limits of popular conscience. People find it reassuring to be made to care about what they thought they already cared about. It is the fertile land of shared perceptions. The Theatre of Conscience is essentially a mass declaration of loyalty to moral principles. But it is not, as I believe art has to be, promiscuous. It is an activity that never sins.

Let me suggest that the theatre is literally a box, physically and morally a box. What occurs in the box is infinite because the audience wishes it to be infinite – there is no burden of proof at any moment. It is a black box, when the lights are off, because, as we all know, darkness permits the criminal and the promiscuous act. I wrote a play called *The Bite of the Night*. Darkness permits the thought, darkness licenses, it bites, and sometimes you can be bitten by love and sometimes by fear. When Brecht commanded that the box be filled with light he was driven by the passion for enlightenment, and he knew instructions require light just as the imagination hates light and flees from it. Imagination also flees its neighbours. In light you are only half-conscious of the stage and half-conscious of your neighbour. In all collective culture your neighbour controls you by his gaze. In darkness he is eliminated and you are alone with the actor. This is why the didactic play occurs in the street – street theatre is about teaching, black box theatre is about imagination. In the black box you are trusted to be free, to be solely responsible. To enter it is to be engulfed by the possibility of freedom through the powers of the actor and the dramatist, the onus is placed on the audience not as a collectivity, but as individuals. No disciplines, no recall to conscience. Because the box is hidden from the world, it owes as little as it wishes to the world, the rules in the box are different from the rules outside it. What else can explain the residual excitement we still experience in dark theatres? Why are we still a little half-afraid? Is it because we are about to watch an actor? Yes, because actors are not entirely human, but more, it is the sense of attending on a sin, the possibility of witnessing a transgression, the freedom to part with the necessary disciplines of the street, the possibility of acquiring that criminal perspective – not more enlightenment, but less. And of course, it is not you who sins, the actors sin for you. The box is a dangerous place, but you are not yourself physically in danger – all theatre that affronts or offends the audience by direct engagement wrecks that sacred compact between actor and witness that is older than history. To insult the audience for the paltry gratification of the actors destroys theatre, erodes its authority as an art, just as all invitations to debate what has been witnessed diminish its beauty. The great play is immune to discussion, the play eliminates debate, it is not about arguments, it replaces arguments.

A drama teacher, a pacifist, visited me. He told me of his production of *Antigone*, in which instead of a set he hung a massive map of the world on which every war currently being fought was illuminated by flaming red light. Of course, there were lots of these, and the actors played in the glare of them. At the end, he flung on the house lights and dragged chairs on to the stage, obliging the audience to engage in a debate on the so-called issues the production had raised. He therefore succeeded in eliminating the entire experience of the drama, humiliated the text by using it as a means to an end, a starting point for the endless curse of debating things, wrecked the invention of his actors, turning them into mere didactic instruments, and liquidated any possibility in the audience that their structure of feeling and thought could be inflamed by what they had witnessed – he had reduced the non-cerebral event of a play into a pack of arguments.

I repeat that the play is not a debate, it is literally 'play', and like children's play it is 'world-inventing', requiring no legitimation from the exterior. It is about impossibilities, and takes its immense spiritual authority from the simple question 'what if . . .?' not from the banal 'did you know . . .?' The question 'what if . . .?' immunizes the theatre from its worst enemies, the material researchers, who can devastate a documentary by flourishing a single fact. In black box theatre nothing can be challenged on the ground that it did not occur, or has no precedent. The response to the plaintive cry 'this could never happen!' is 'precisely, we are playing a play!' And play is dangerous, of course, it goes where it is not expected to go, it is quite simply immoral. When Hochhuth wrote his notorious play on Winston Churchill, the work was obscured – or it was intended to be – by a massive correspondence about the Churchillian archives. Hochhuth had 'researched' his play, but never well enough. By his meticulous realist method, he robbed his chosen art form of its major resource, and the whole event shifted from inside the theatre to outside it, to the columns of newspapers. If writers use theatre only as a means to get access to newspaper columns – what they call initiating debate – they vandalize theatre, they tear gaping holes in its walls through which a miserable daylight streams, showing us that actors are, after all, only people with painted faces.

It is my contention that theatre's power in the contemporary world ought to be much greater than it is, but that it has wilfully chosen to emasculate itself by imitating the habits of its rivals. Its writers are smitten with the idea of themselves as educators, and have subordinated actors to their wishes. They have made a theatre of morals almost as rigid as the medieval stage and have contributed to a new style of social conformism. They have told what they know, and have not dared to tread where they do not know, which is the authentic territory of a black box theatre. I also am a moralist, but not a puritan. By moralist I mean one who is tough with morality, who exposes it to risk, even to oblivion, and it is not for nothing I chose the theatre as my field because in essence the theatre is not a moral place, as our ancestors knew well when they intermittently banned it. It is a long time since anyone wanted to ban the theatre in this country, and that is itself suggestive. It is responsible, it is loyal, it is a willing collaborator in the enforcing of moral regulations. Let me for the last time return to the writer who thinks the purpose of his life and art is 'to make people understand one another'. I must admit that for many years when people asked me why I wrote, I resorted to such dismal platitudes myself, though with a deep sense of bad faith. I had a sense that art was a luxury and needed to be defended against charges of indulgence or privilege. In fact, I wrote because I needed to. I wrote for myself. But that seemed unforgivable. Only more recently did I understand that in writing for myself I also served others, and that, in not serving myself, I could not serve others. The more self-limiting an artist is, the less useful to his fellow human beings; the more he dares, the more he explores, and the

[76]

more immoral he is, the better he serves. Then he or she becomes the enemy of collective lying. Then he or she runs the risk of seeing the work denied. Great art lives outside the moral system, and its audience, consciously or unconsciously, demands it, particularly in theatre whose very darkness is the condition of a secret pact, the pact of wilful infringement, of the suspension of conscience, between actor and audience. And the actor, as I suggested earlier, is not entirely human, nor do we wish him to be. He is not – and here as in most ways I totally reject the principles of community theatre – merely someone who might be in the audience on another night, the grocer in a funny hat, or your uncle pretending to be your ancestor – but quite other than us, gifted in special ways, not least in body and speech, particularly in speech; he has the gift of seducing – after all, dance is permitted everywhere, dance is the conformist act and ironically, repressive – but speech, that is the lost secret, and poetic speech is nearly religious in its power: not the humdrum repetition of naturalistic drama, but the rhythmic, undulating, journey of the articulated form known as 'the speech'. On the stage the actor is licensed to do the undoable, and he or she 'takes us out of ourselves' – a strangely accurate phrase that, like most common expressions, hides as much as it reveals. To be 'taken out of yourself' – the very thing demanded of the actor – is to be like the dog let off its lead, the lead being conscience, the lead being responsibility and loyalty. Like the dog, the actor experiences an atavistic moment of relief, wildness and barbarism, and even fear – for he is domesticated, after all – so we glimpse, with fear and delight, the landscape of a pre-moral world and are allowed to run in it. And what is the form of this landscape, for there is only one? It is tragedy. Impossible in comedy, for comedy is the suspension, the denial of emotion. The artist who dares to be tragic, the actor who is unafraid of tragedy, lives at the expense of his conscience, lives outside conscience. He sins for the audience, living on the very fringes of morality. This is the reason the actor in historic periods was banned, even in death, from hallowed ground – he was the player of the forbidden action, the manifestation of forbidden life. In a conscience-free theatre, there is, of course, no 'telling'. It is the farthest reach from the Brechtian demonstration. There is no 'telling' because the writer had nothing to tell – his play was a journey to him as it is a journey to the actor, the outcome of which was unknown at its beginning. It was for the writer a journey without maps whose destination might be an intemperate zone, a place of fear and little comfort. This is the very act of honouring that I have described elsewhere – the honouring of an audience by refusing the simple satisfactions of reiteration, affirmations, congratulation – the sort of theatre in which the morality was fixed in advance, and the writing, and the narrative was a means to an end. I repeat that the theatre tells nothing, and in a society where telling never stops, where news, political comment, advertising, the social debate, are a deafening cacophony, an orchestra of claims and counter-claims, all subject to the moral consensus of humanism, the theatre's sole and riveting power lies in its barbarism. Against the walls of the theatre there washes continuously the sea of morality and debate. The walls protect the actor and the audience not only from the racket of the street but also from its morality. Inside the black box, the imagination is wild and tragic and its criminality unfettered. The unspeakable is spoken. Here alone is the audience trusted with the full burden of what it has witnessed and liberated from the ideology of redemption, it witnesses in silence, a silence of pain, the terrible ambitions of the human spirit. Cruelty. Magnificence. Wrong actions. Instinct. Horror. Love beyond legality. When an audience witnesses such things beyond the structures of redemption or education, ideology or affirmation, it has recourse only to silence, a pathos which is perhaps a kind of self-pity permitted to a hero who finds himself, at last, alone.

The deconsecration of meaning in the Theatre of Catastrophe

The Theatre of Catastrophe refuses to endorse clarity as a principle of production in art. The question 'What is he saying?' cannot be applied to this theatre and is already a form of decadence. In this theatre the idea of 'saying' is redundant, just as the idea of clarity is seen to harbour an authoritarianism. In its place, we aim for a multiplicity of effects and a different form of theatrical experience. In this theatre the judgement that 'this play appears to have no meaning' is not felt as criticism. A new relation is forged between the audience and the stage which abolishes the idea of entertainment and the oppressive intellectual practices that this concept entails. Why have we come to this conclusion?

Firstly, the expectations aroused by three decades of political theatre have produced an intellectual servility in audiences. This servility is expressed in the desperate ache for the message, which denigrates the experience of art. Where the message is not evident the audience becomes resentful and the actors a target of contempt. This relation of audience and stage is a corrupt one since it implies knowledge to be a commodity, given by the dramatist to a fee-paying class.

Secondly, the discipline of political theatre eliminates complexity and contradiction, and massages its audience towards a futile celebration of prior knowledge. I mean by this the hidden assumption of shared morality which lies behind, for example, the idea of exposure. The political play has been relentless in its pursuit of exposure, the unveiling of conspiracies, the comic denigration of social types, political parties, etc., all of this resting on the sterile belief in a common morality, liberal-humanist, left-leaning, socially progressive.

Thirdly, the emphasis on clarity and realism has effectively abolished poetry from the stage, thereby colluding in the disfigurement of speech in the public arena and enthroning the journalist as the proprietor of truth. The theatre of clarity distrusts the audience it claims to serve, by denying them the right to experience the meaningless.

I want to discuss the idea of the meaningless play with reference to a number of works of my own produced principally by The Wrestling School or the Almeida Theatre, *The Possibilities*, *The Last Supper*, *Seven Lears*, but also some produced by national companies like the Royal Shakespeare such as *The Castle* and *The Bite of the Night*. These are the more recent plays in what I have characterized as a Theatre of Catastrophe, but some of the qualities of this type of drama are to be found in much earlier work, work which I believed at the time possessed a didactic or critical purpose.

What these plays have in common is their indigestibility. For all that they possess in terms of classic dramatic values, such as narrative, structure, character or language, they are irreducible to a set of meanings. The parables in *The Last Supper* and the ten plays of *The Possibilities* are not construable. This is not to say they are incomprehensible. They are merely narratives whose linkage to agreed moral structures is ruptured. This moral compact which has dominated the aesthetic environment of theatre in the last thirty years is abolished in the Theatre of Catastrophe and opens the prospect of a new relationship between the audience and the stage.

What do I think this relationship is, and how do I think it should be different? It is my judgement that the weakness of the contemporary theatre is its fear of the audience. The raked seating of most auditoria evokes the lecture hall or, worse, the jury box. The gratification of this potentially hostile mass, ranked above the actors in a position of critical dominance, is the first function of the performance. Leaving aside the commercial theatre, the idea of 'the success', even among radical companies, induces a predisposition to make compromises with the fullest demands of creative imagination which in theatre, as in any art, requires absolute licence. The horror that 'they' may not 'understand' the scene, that 'they' may lose the thread of the narrative, or that 'we' shall be accused of elitism if 'meaning' becomes obscure – and how this word 'obscure' is used to beat writers over the head – cripples the theatre with its false democracy. It is my view that behind the notions of 'clarity' and 'meaning' lies a contempt both for the audience and for the powers of imagination.

The disintegration of the liberal-humanist consensus offers scope for altering this governing aesthetic of production. In an age of excess, of entertainment, information, documentation and analysis, the theatre gains nothing by competing with superior technologies. A theatre of social analysis, dependent on the communication of ideas and, consequently, on a permanent narrative of meaning, treats its audience like a dog on a lead. The terror felt by an audience deprived of such a narrative is akin to the shock felt by an animal uncaged – it is hesitant, even resistant, to the prospect of its own freedom. In the Theatre of Catastrophe the deal under which the audience resigns its rights to the domination of the author in exchange for information or entertainment, conscience or massage, is abolished. The first signal that no such compact exists comes from the unfamiliar cadences of a new language, whose rhythms and syntax are not those of common speech. It is a speech as contrived as poetry, dislocated, sometimes lyrical, often coarse, whose density and internal contradictions both evoke and confuse. In a culture in which language has lost its public status in favour of image and selling, this flood of verbal sound overwhelms the listener, who must be content with a partial understanding but whose attention is fixed by the sensuality of substance of speech in the mouth of the trained actor. It has been often remarked that my theatre is predominantly an actors' theatre, and it is certainly true that actors have been my greatest allies and collaborators. This reflects the supreme responsibility that is placed in them, in their powers of articulation to conduct what is in effect a symphony of speech. It is this displacement of attention from meaning to texture that characterizes the first moments of the play. The actors' seduction of the audience, which, as in any seduction, is achieved by means other than the rational, is crucial to the renewal of, and the renegotiation of, the terms of the theatre.

I have said that the existing theatre, with its configuration of stage and seating, inhibits the unblocking of imagination by its mute assertion of power. By collectively situating the audience in blocks who peer into the pit of the stage, or even gaze down a raked landscape of seats, this is a theatre which implies a unanimity of response. I have said elsewhere that one of the most depressing sounds in the theatre is that of the audience in the unified pursuit of a single goal – the laugh, for example – which is so easily achieved. I regard this as an essentially servile relationship on both sides of the lights – the performers and authors who are gratified to have struck a seam of unanimity – and the audience who sense they have achieved value for money. A more complex and creative theatre uses moments of unanimity only to achieve more startling effects of division, in

[81]

which the audience is atomized and in which the laugh, where it occurs, is accompanied by a sense of the faux pas, or where it comes unbidden, from amazement that comedy exists at all. The possibility of the audience feeling itself at liberty to respond individually to what it witnesses – its liberation from the shackles of meaning – can be properly cultivated only in a theatre which is not one.

Our task is to make theatre a necessity. This can be achieved only when what it provides ceases to be entertainment on the one hand, or moral or political instruction on the other. In the Theatre of Catastrophe its powers of reconciliation or resolution are abolished in favour of a passionate assertion of human complexity which cannot be distorted by ideology or shaped by the goodwill of humanist collectivity. The new audience that has appeared for this theatre is not oppressed by the absence of meaning or the threat of obscurity. Both these terms, along with the accusation of pessimism, are regarded by such an audience as critical barriers erected to sustain the existing economy of stage/audience relations. We live in an age of persistent meaning, of relentless indoctrination, not only from the state, but from the artistic community, the commercial empires and the propagandist forces of an information network. The status of news – which includes opinion – has never been greater. The theatre must resolutely defy the persuasive logic of news and return the rights of interpretation to the audience. In this freedom from the oppression of meaning audiences will discover the necessity of theatre as a multitude of possibilities in which the constant imperative of judgement is willingly surrendered.

When I talked to an audience of students after the first performance of *The Last Supper* in 1988, I was subjected to a tirade of abuse from a young man who had found the evening deeply discomforting. This abuse was directed at me, and not at the actors, whose performances, he was compelled to admit, were beyond reproach. The substance of his complaint was that he felt foolish, and was humiliated, by the absence of meaning in the play. His intellect, trained in methods of analysis, and his experience, formed from the endless narratives of televisual realism, rebelled against the play's deflective surfaces. He had paid money to be taught, and the actors had taught him nothing, other than the power of acting. At least, so it appeared to him. I argued that this anger, which in its violence revealed profound disturbance, was a symptom of a struggle he was obliged to undertake to emerge from a servile relationship he experienced with theatre, from which he demanded product in the form of knowing where I stood. Once he knew where I stood, he would be satisfied. I could not say where I stood. As long as I had known where I stood, I produced inferior theatre, intent on demonstrating my thesis. Instead I offered in this play the experience, which was itself the purpose of the evening's work. And I use the word *work* deliberately, since the work is not only the actors', but also the audience's. The play is a landscape in which the audience is encouraged to wander without maps. It is marked, it is not chaotic, but the disciplines of this theatre do not include the disciplines of demonstration. I am glad to say this student's bitterness was not common to the others. Many said they abandoned, or struggled to abandon, their demands, early in the play, some as soon as the invitation arrived in the form of the prologue. Once this discarding had occurred, they were able to immerse themselves in the actions, moving from scene to scene fluidly, refusing to be stuck on points of loss or obvious contradiction. In this they found an appetite for theatre which was not diminished by the fact that they made no claim to 'understand' it. Because we played in a conventional theatre, this movement was harder to achieve. Physically they had encountered the play in seats, pampered as consumers. They had not expected to work, let alone to suffer. Everything conspired to make them pass judgement on what failed to entertain them. They overcame these conditions in an alliance with a company of actors whose faith was infectious.

For the theatre to regain the initiative in a society which offers a superfluity of dramatic product it must address itself to its own uniqueness. This entails the creation of structures in both language and narrative that do not owe their legitimacy to representation of the world beyond the stage. The audience must feel what it witnesses is beyond what it conceives to be common experience. In my play *The Bite of the Night* a classics teacher at a defunct university, having driven his father to suicide and his son into vagrancy, takes his favoured pupil Hogbin on a reluctant tour of the Eleven Troys of antiquity, engaging with Helen in a succession of political systems each of which reduces her physically until she is no more than a voice in a chair. The ahistoricity of this journey is obvious, the collapsing of time and narrative signalling to the audience that it must forsake its conventional expectations of meaning, and the interventions of scenes of interlude which bear only obliquely on the main action, encouraging it to suspend its urge to organize the material until the conclusion of the performance. Beyond this, each act of this three-act play opens with a prologue whose poetic discursiveness lends only the most slender connections in terms of meaning to the act about to follow, but which draw the audience further away from its organizational instincts into a form of surrender to an intensity of dramatic experience which stimulates its imaginative involvement to a point at which it is overwhelmed. This play has a performance time of about five hours. The Royal Shakespeare Company felt it necessary to issue an apology for the length of this experience, thereby confessing its inability to trust theatre when it failed to commoditize itself properly. In its struggle to contain the power of drama in its contest with the greater conveniences of television or film, the State theatre condemns theatre to irrelevance, eroding the very bases of its uniqueness.

The cult of accessibility and the Theatre of Obscurity

There are two critical terms which have become, in regard to my own work, the definitive signals of approval or hostility. One of these is a neologism, the other is as old as criticism itself. One is a catchword of a corrupt political culture and the other a respectable concept which has been annexed in a desperate search for a derogatory terminology. I refer to those two poles of contemporary judgement, accessibility and obscurity.

The first of these is by no means limited to theatre, or even to art itself. We hear about the need for 'access' to museums, 'access' to spaces, 'access' to the countryside, to education, to information, even to knowledge itself. There is nothing, apparently, to which 'access' cannot be applied. This liberal-sounding criterion conceals a profound suspicion of the imagination behind a fashionable hatred of privilege. All things that are not accessible must be privileged, the theory runs, all spaces that are hidden are ipso facto the preserves of an elite, and all ideas or works of art that fail to communicate themselves are – obscure. In this sham democracy, it is not only the entire stock of the culture that must be thrown open, or vilified, there is an obligation laid on the living artist to make himself 'understood'. Thus with regard to my own work, the play which receives the approval of the critical regime is first and foremost the 'accessible' one, whose narrative is simple, whose characters are rapidly absorbed, identified and classified as 'good' or 'bad', and whose momentum can be contained within the 'issue', in this case the 'issue' of artistic freedom and State patronage. This constricting and oppressive critical straitjacket, with its hatred for abstraction, threatens writers, musicians, museum administrators and doubtless, in future, philosophers, too.

Those who are threatened by the dictat of accessibility, 'Be understood or Perish', need to keep their nerve, since in a populist culture the abuse from certain quarters is bound to become increasingly violent. The writer of 'inaccessible' theatre will be repudiated

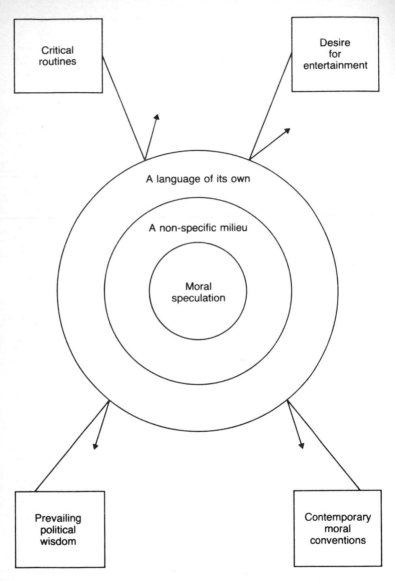

Plan for the fortification of an imaginative work

as a poseur, or, most favoured of all English calumnies, identified as 'pretentious'. His collaborators will be seen as dupes, the actors vilified as brainless exhibitionists, and the institution which mounts the production attacked as corrupt, elitist and overdue for demolition.

Theatrical experience as pure commodity entails frontal attacks of this kind on all work which does not yield instant meaning, meaning which is frequently no more than narrative itself – hence the emphasis on 'structure' in reactionary practice, 'real life' and such-like. The theatre's historic bondage to the idea of 'entertainment' has ensured that alternative experiences of theatre lack even a proper vocabulary for their expression. We have all experienced the conversation which begins 'Did you enoy that play . . . ?' and the response, 'Well, I don't think *enjoy* is exactly the word . . .', but what is the word? The accessible play poses no such problems for the critic or the audience. Its problem and its solution are one and the same. It reiterates the conventional opinion much as my own play *Scenes from an Execution* reiterates the belief that artists tell the truth, a very dubious and, of course, circular opinion. What this play, and all 'accessible' plays, do is to exist within moral certitudes. I think it is safe to say that no accessible play denies the moral burden of the climate in which it is created. In its exigesis it affirms the reigning moral consensus, no matter what the shocks it delivers en route. In this fatal bond between imagination and existent morality, the play about 'issues' becomes the most 'relevant', 'important' and 'accessible' of all theatre, since it can operate only in a field of shared morality. Michael Billington, a critic more obsessed with the accessible than most, forlornly pleads that I should address myself to 'contemporary issues', as if here, at least, consensus must be restored. Here is articulated – out of despair at 'obscurity' – the suffocating insistence of liberal-humanist ideological solidarity.

Accessibility demands that whatever our differences we must speak a common tongue (usually street naturalism) and share a common morality. It also invites, without necessarily stating the necessity for, the old reactionary quality of celebration. But what about a theatre that repudiates this? Or indeed any art that declines to share in the governing notions of 'goodness', 'importance' or 'relevance'? What are its characteristics? The first will be – yes – its 'obscurity'. For such a theatre will hardly announce itself in terms of clarity, since nothing is clear here, least of all morality. And, yes, the author will certainly not be in 'command of his material', most of which will be – yes – 'undigested'. His thoughts will certainly be disorganized, and he will certainly appear 'not to know what he is doing'. He will not know how to structure a play, let alone make it well-made, and, what is more, will, in a spasm of shocking elitism, appear to be 'wrestling with his own demons', the very antithesis of the accessible play, where authors grapple with everybody else's demons. This is the theatre of selfishness, and its maker is someone who sees himself or herself unashamedly as an artist, the power of whose imagination is their sole claim on public attention. This is a theatre whose business is not 'communication' at all, but expression. To the pains and triumphs of this instinct which makes no compromise with moral responsibility, an audience comes which demands the very thing in shortest supply in a populist regime of culture – complexity, contradiction, pain and absence – the precious silence born of the absence of both solutions and moral exhortation. In this theatre all is obscurity, since nothing is known, it is relentlessly speculative, and its judgements are made, if at all, in the days and weeks following performance, never in the experience itself.

In this theatre also, the ingrained habits of seeing and hearing as a means to the construction of meaning are suspended – and surprisingly easily for many people. Images are relished for themselves, and language becomes a sensuality, like the voice of the actor itself. The entire onus of meaning, the super-objective of the Stanislavsky school, is displaced from the stage on to the audience which feels either betrayed or exhilarated; cheated or honoured; tricked out of its conventional rewards or looted in the private recesses of its soul. 'What did it mean . . . ?' – that melancholy cry of an audience sent away without its message or the satisfaction of seeing 'real life' – is discovered to be an archaic question, a rudimentary response to a cultural oppression, or a populist spasm of amour-propre on the part of an audience whose members until then have liked to think of artists as 'just like them', articulators of their problems and witnesses of their lives.

I have called this a Theatre of Catastrophe, but it might as well be a Theatre of Obscurity in its abolition of the moral compact which underlies the 'accessible' play. It is a theatre of powerful disciplines, nevertheless, and by no means a torrent of unconsciousness. Very obvious transgressions occur which make it deeply unsympathetic to existing practice – the first of these being its irresponsibility. It is one of the planks of a liberal-humanist theatre that its artists are responsible, men and women of conscience and social purpose. I am bound to say the exclusion of my work from the National Theatre of England in the past 18 years can only reflect its hidden moral function – common to all national theatres by definition – 'the serving of the community', as if the community were served by conscience in the first place. It is certainly one of the flawed conventions of my accessible play *Scenes from an Execution* that the protagonist, the artist Galactia, with whom all critics find it easy to sympathize, is a pacifist. I am inclined to wonder how the play might have been received if I had had the courage and imagination to present her as an apologist for violence. I have another play, *The Bite of the Night*, in which the protagonist incites his father to suicide and collaborates in the dismemberment of a woman, Helen of Troy. This play is described by Michael Billington as 'enragingly obscure'. Let the first rule of the Obscure Theatre therefore be its repudiation of virtue, that debilitating sense that the author is 'on our side', 'one of us', and ready and willing to 'nail the enemy', with his persistent wit.

The pleasures of the Obscure Theatre are, I suggest, to be found in precisely those areas which give rise to such anxiety amongst the lovers of accessibility, and the conflict I have attempted to outline is a long and fundamental quarrel over the nature and function of art itself. The common aspiration of every writer in every medium is that his work should 'create new perceptions'. This weary formula sounds less convincing with every telling. What does it mean, and how does this peculiar phenomenon occur? If it does occur, how can it be compatible with 'access'? I cannot for a moment pretend I have ever written for a public whom I judged in need of enlightenment. I have never wanted to 'tell' anything to anyone, or wished to alter their views on any subject. I was always engaged with the problems of my own psyche and the tensions within my own personality. The theatre I have chosen to embrace is one which makes no compact with its audience as to entertainment, ideological instruction, humanist celebration or changed perceptions. As the artist chiefly responsible for what occurs on the stage I claim no superior insight or even the status of a visionary, let alone a just man with a conscience. My obscurity is precisely the result of sacrificing these claims to attention, and an act of pure irresponsibility, and I justify my theatre not by its contribution to a humanist culture – a celebration of the essential goodness of the man animal – but precisely by its suspension of morality. There are no good people in these plays, nor is happiness posited as an end at all; reconciliation fails to arrive, or is disrupted, and love is a manifestation of cruelty. In this apparent pessimism, which is pessimism only to those schooled in the official doctrine of optimism, the appeal can never be to conscience, but only to the undeniable power of pain in the imagination, the play being open not to a single interpretation, but to many, with the resulting appetite for re-viewing which characterizes the audience of this work. No one sees *Scenes from an Execution* twice, but they come back to *Seven Lears*, as they returned to *The Bite of the Night*, not in search of the meaning I have hidden in the undergrowth of the text, but to make it for themselves. For them, 'accessibility' is now the tedium of a servile art.

A bargain with impossibility:
the theatre of moral speculation
in an age of accord*

One of the uglier clichés of artistic production in a culture such as ours is the routine justification of effort by results. The complicity between artist and critic achieves an unhealthy apotheosis in the reiteration of the phrase – invented to sustain a dominant cultural myth – that such and such a work of art 'changed perceptions', as if in some delightfully painless way society edged towards ever greater civility by virtue of watching plays or observing pictures. You can hear this uttered as both the ultimate critical accolade, and the self-conscious artist's anxious plea for justification in an age of relentless utilitarianism. If his duty is to entertain, his reward is the knowledge that his dramatic skills inflicted upon his audience some collective shift of focus. But what does it mean, this labouring to 'change perceptions'? It serves to incorporate artists and actors into a social consensus of conscience and critique, and bestows on them a spurious respectability – it is redolent of earnestness, responsibility, legislative/poetic romanticism, the sort of fake heroism that now attaches to journalists of the investigative kind and has infected drama with its relentless exposés of yet further scandals that merely confirm – what? – our mutual fascination with corruption? our common desire to humiliate the rich? Dramatists may pursue the fallacy of 'changed perceptions' to a point of exhaustion – except that there is no point of exhaustion in an art which is both inspired and justified by the desire to affirm a popular morality. Man is the social animal whose antics reward permanent observation, but the price of an art of conscience is a stage peopled by characters who cannot achieve autonomy, and therefore do not operate at the imaginative level – they are observed, not invented. There is great safety and security to be enjoyed in the exchange of conscience-ridden observations, affirmations of shared values, humanistic platitudes, but the

* George Orwell Memorial Lecture, Birkbeck College, 4 December 1991.

stage remains essentially sterile, and the insistence on the representation of what passes for the real world only enhances the decadent sense of social responsibility whilst devastating the landscape of dramatic invention.

The entire spectrum of theatre is susceptible to this culture of justification by results, the utilization for collectively respectable ends of an art form once suspiciously irrational in its origins and effects, and this annexation has its origins in Shaw, Brecht and the Enlightenment dramatists like Lessing. We now enjoy a unanimity of functional intention that extends from the wildest performance arts to the most highly-invested language theatre of the National – the cultural accord is total. The well-intentioned children of the Welfare State have grown into cultural producers of social critiques for both mass and minority audiences. Behind their spectacular or routine dramatic methods lies the spectacle of relentless harmony – it has become impossible any longer actually to *resent* the artistic experience, to feel any resistance to it per se, since like Chekhov's character Astrov in *Uncle Vanya* it is so profoundly permeated with idealism that dissonance is prostrated. Who could disagree that we are living an ecological disaster? Who would choose to defend the legal profession or the art market? We swim a tepid bath of humanistic accord, writer, actor, audience, an alliance of foregone conclusions which diminishes the possibility of innovative practice.

What I am describing is in effect a collusion between the populist State – defined by the near-identity of the political programme no matter which party articulates it – and a theatre no longer able to live its radical functions as they were expressed, say, in the 1960s and 1970s – a theatre which prided itself on its contribution to a debate, and fatally diminished itself in the process. What we now witness is such an accord between art and society that it is impossible to distinguish (in moral terms) the work of grossly over-funded national theatres – which are simply artistic arms of the national conscience – and the theatre of the margins. The drama of conscience reigns virtually unopposed, and the aspiration to 'change perceptions' is welcome on all sides of the political spectrum – if it is a spectrum at all. It is a further aspect of modern populism that everyone is entitled to complain at injustice, even to pursue it in the full glare of publicity, and the clean sweep of the humanist regime incorporates entertainers and critics alike. In a drama emerging from a process of empirical research, the source of inspiration is inevitably indignation

[92]

at malpractice, and there is neither a threat to order nor, more significantly, any possible extension of experience in a realist project of this kind. What occurs is the routine massaging of collective values that passes for 'communication', communication being territorial familiarity, acts of recognition, the stimulation of sympathy with the catalogue of known and revered victims. It is a theatre whose heroic period consisted in the annexation of common experience, but whose decadence consists in its fixed embrace of common morality.

I would like to propose a different theatre, in which conscience is removed from its dominant function and criticism is confined to that fatal axis where it alone operates to the common good – that which lies between the artist and the text, the self-criticism exercised in deletion, excision, self-denial of the banal and the routine. I would like to propose that the value of works of art, in social circumstances such as the present, lies not in their entertainment value, nor in their ability to 'change perceptions' in pursuit of some common purpose, but in their power to devastate the received wisdom of the collective, which conspires to diminish individual experience at all levels. A theatre which addresses the individual and ceases to regard the audience as an entity, which denies the existence of the audience as singular at all, must above all things be irresponsible and disloyal. It cannot hope for the status of social critic, since the social critic is fully incorporated, and it must not clamour for the comforts of solidarity, the much-vaunted 'celebration' of the community play or the musical, for these are the realm of the commercial or the politically facile. It is in the rupturing of these ties – essentially the breaking of the curse of entertainment – that the prospect of a new theatre lies. Formal innovations in theatre – the slide towards anti-literary theatre, anti-linguistic theatre – will not solve what is, in essence, an impasse created by excessive harmony. The action of such a form of drama will not be to labour to 'widen sympathy' or 'to make us understand one another better', another element of the catechism of the humanist theatre, but rather the opposite, to engender division, to weaken spurious ties, to provoke a sense of incurable alienation from the polis which alone can give us access to the authentic experience of tragedy – for the pursuit of harmony and unity (the sentimental ambition of artists and, to some extent, their sole licence) abolished tragedy in the fond pursuit of rational order and spiritual peace. The relations of such a radical theatre with the 'real world' – observed reality and common territory – are not those of the documentary observer who hauls on to the stage – and in daylight, by theory – the 'problem' or the 'issue' of a given subject, but are fugitive from it and in pursuit of the hidden, the unarticulated material of the psyche where it *confronts* reality. It is primarily a speculative art – a bargain with impossibility – since it is not subject to empirical truth and denies the critique of realism at every turn. The power of conviction in writer and performer are its own justifications, enabling individuals in the audience to cross the threshold of reality principles and trespass where morality is insecure. The bargain between the stage and the audience is struck not a priori by common principles but between individuals in pursuit of imaginative reconnoitre. This crucial point of rupture with governing principles of politics and morality is its distinguishing characteristic, and it entails – something I am not able to enter into here – new manners of performance since the governing models of the contemporary theatre – still wholly Stanislavskian and Brechtian in nature – are rigorously anti-speculative, obsessed with intentions and objectives, and oppressive in their severe delimitations of stage action and actors' invention.

The title of this paper, 'A bargain with impossibility', derives from a poem written by me in response to an incident that occurred here at Birkbeck some years ago following the showing of my television play *Pity in History*. It refers to the compact which exists between an imaginative art and its audience. The reaction of an old soldier, who appeared to have wandered in from the street, bedecked with medals which clearly demonstrated his rights to his own history – his empirical authority, so to speak, to debate the subject of war and injury – was profoundly hostile to the portrayal of a dying army cook played – with characteristic energy – by the actor Ian McDiarmid. This old soldier's bitterness underlined for me the poverty of the common perception of theatre and its responsibilities that now dominates the realist discourse. The poem, which is titled 'Men don't die like that', takes this rebuke as its starting point.

Men don't die like that

The tramp would thrash me with his memory
For showing death like this*
Would lay his scourge of anger down my back

[94]

Ten for impertinence
Ten for irreverence
Ten for failing to observe the facts

His medals jangle like drunk girls
His grave mouth gapes for oaths to
Satisfy a violated piety

Suffering lends him authority which he
Transports like an archbishop's hat

He knows
He saw
He yells

Men don't die like that

No use pleading my method
To list theatre's bargains with impossibility
Would be a waste of breath
This high priest of experience can't be gainsaid
He swings his pain over my head

The
    Unrepentant
        Stager
           Of
              Discord

  For I

Though my speculation cruelly offends
Concede nothing to the recollectionist
Knowing fidelity would pulp the heart of art
More savagely than shells did his friends

Decades of naturalistic drama – and the political and social values that attach to it – had taught this individual member of the audience that the sole purpose of showing an action on stage was to achieve the highest proximity to human experience, and that any deviation from it constituted an offence against the collective – was in effect, lying. What I was groping towards in plays of that period within the body of my own work was an emphatic disassociation, a rupture, between stage and reality, in effect a licence to lie, which had,

---

* *Pity in History*, BBC TV, 1985.

indeed, long existed in the history of the theatre but which had been revoked. I wanted to take advantage of fiction, to permit more articulation than nature would permit, simply, to *exaggerate*, and to do so with a form of language that was – despite the actor's ease – contrived, dense, poetic, in a way common speech rarely can be, so both the content and the mode of expression were unhindered by considerations of truth-to-life. This, of course, is no more than a description of dramatic method before the nineteenth century, but there are times when the reoccupation of abandoned aesthetic territory is the point of departure for more significant developments.

If the Theatre of Conscience and Criticism – as I think one might characterize the best post-war British theatre – renounced poetic language as artificial, it also attempted to demolish the walls of the theatre, a laudable enough aim when those walls filtered pain from patrons bent on escapism and the perpetuation of images of leisured life – when they were, in effect, protecting the audience from experience by reproducing the ethic of drawing-room society. But nothing is immune from its own processes of decay, and it is my contention that a theatre without walls, a theatre which – metaphorically – exists in the street, having once liberated imagination, now stifles it, and that the fact of its privileged space is now its greatest lever on curiosity, and both its walls and darkness permit a freedom from the moral consensus not tolerated elsewhere. To persist with the metaphor, the walls symbolically and actually define freedom within, and the darkness permits precisely the atomization of the audience that Brecht so longed to forbid, preferring *his* audience to sit in white light and thereby discipline and educate each other, under the enlightened control of the author. The bargain I want to define is therefore one in which the audience individual demands of the dramatist not the reiteration of collective values, the narrative which is suspended from the threads of popularly held beliefs, but the relentless speculation on morality which touches only at points on the familiar, which invokes the real world only in order to dislocate it. This is the country of Obscurity where the common equipment of critical judgement – at least as understood in the contemporary theatre – finds no place. The criteria of the humanist critic, related almost entirely to utilitarian standards – mutual understanding, social benefit, enhancement of life within certain narrow boundaries – can no more apply to a theatre of this kind than can an actor trained in naturalistic techniques and nurtured on televisual realism perform its language. It is, in its first principles, a theatre which invents a world rather than representing one, and it is, furthermore, relentlessly tragic. In other words, it is a theatre of pain, but one without obligations to reconciliation or harmony.

Tragedy is possible only in cultures secure enough to tolerate the performance of infringements against collective wisdom. Insecure cultures shelter in the penumbra of moral certainty, reiterated with diminishing conviction on stages of extreme moral propriety – is it possible to conceive of a theatre more fixed and sclerotic with propriety than the National Theatre of England? This propriety is, of course, characterized by an adherence to the socio-critical play, whether it is a routine revival of Fo's *Accidental Death* or star vehicle texts like Brecht's *Arturo Ui* whose satirical targets are safely confined to the nostalgic era, and it is perhaps hardly worth making the observation that national theatres reproduce national ideologies, whatever idealist propaganda may have attended on their births. My point is a simple one, that the breadth of the moral compact, which is itself a sign of profound social unease, makes the writing of tragedy an act of *lèse majesté*; the imagining of the forbidden, with the aesthetic principles that might accompany it – invented language, speeches whose content is destabilizing of the actor's conventional method, being digressionary, contradictory within the span of a sentence, and with no objectives at all – is the negation of naturalism, the negation of satire, of cheer-leading, enemy-identifying and, above all, the negation of the post-Chekhovian, suburban self-hatred that permeates late humanist theatre at this time in this country.

A theatre of tragedy makes its end the very opposite of the end of entertainment – it complicates life, and sends its audience away with that faint grudge at having been troubled at a level beneath the consciously moral. It displaces the simple gratifications of 'A good night out', and insists on the exposure of pain that is not soluble. It makes no attempt to 'change perceptions' at all, not regarding that as its business, but arrives at the compact with its audience from a different perspective, that of the deal struck between writer and audience that here at least nothing will be banned, in the interests of either taste or unity, nor will the illicit thought be so treated in dramatic terms as to enable us to dispose of it. There will be no enlightenment dispensed. It is *transgression* that lies at the heart of tragic experience, not accident; it is Lear's howling rebukes to a world without morality that excite us, not his civilizing; it is the heroic actions of his misjudgement that excite our curiosity and not his apology – a dénouement that is the exercise of Christian charity, and an act of will, just as the bloody conclusions of so many Jacobean tragedies are no more than the genuflection of imagination to legality, a debt paid by an artist to a semi-tolerant State.

It is this relation between the dreamer and the State that forms the subject of my own play *The Europeans*, commissioned by the Royal Shakespeare Company in 1985 and due to receive its first professional performance in a production by The Wrestling School in 1993. Set in the liberated Austria of 1683, and taking as its background the struggle in Central Europe against Islamic imperialism, the protagonist is the victim of an atrocity who refuses to forgive, and in her intrepid will to live her pain in public profoundly offends the reconciliatory State. She is a screaming exhibit in the Museum of Reconciliation. The following speech is delivered on a wasteland near Vienna where a youthful bishop has been discovered in the act of burying the body of his mother, whom he has just murdered. The Empress of Austria, a woman of profound curiosity, insists he justifies the act of matricide by preaching a sermon to the assembled labourers and troops.

> The MEN *reluctantly form a circle.* ORPHULS *prepares, and then with the force of inspiration, turns to deliver his oration.*

ORPHULS. All that occurs, does it not occur that I should be its beneficiary, nourished on it, be it filth or excellence? Even the death of love is food to the soul and therefore what is evil? Is there evil except not to do? I do not blaspheme when I say the gift of life is paltry and our best service to God is not to thank Him, endless thanking, no, but to enhance His offer, and yet you do not, I think if I were God I would declare with some weariness or even vehemence, how little they do with the breath I gave them, they exhale repetitions, they applaud the lie, they sleep even in their waking hours, why did I make them thus, I erred in some respect, they fill me with disgust, have you no notion of God's horror? I am thinking of the God in us whose profound groan is the background to our clatter – (*He identifies one of the uncomprehending* WORKMEN.) You shake your head in silence, is that freedom? If silence was freedom it is so no longer, the word is volatile, am I too difficult for you? **Liar! You hide behind the so-called simplicity of Christ, but is that not a blasphemy?** (*Pause.*) If I had not done evil, how could I address you who have perhaps thought evil only? If I did not know cruelty could I know pity, they are the twin towers of the soul? Do not hold hands in false gestures as if by crowding you could exclude the groan of God, no, you must hear the sound of His despair, and we must learn from Judas whose Gospel is not written, we must learn from him who stood alone, for Judas did not sell Christ nor was he corrupt, but Judas was cruel for knowledge, and without Judas there could be no resurrection, Beauty, Cruelty, and Knowledge, these are the triple order of the Groaning God, I speak as your adviser in whose pain you may see beauty, I praise my beauty and you must praise yours! (*Pause.*) I end here, in a proper and terrible exhaustion, I have laid myself before you, which is the duty of a priest. (*Pause.*)

EMPRESS. How wonderful you are . . . I shall not forget one word you said. How wonderful you are, I could truly love you. But we can't know that, and you must die . . . mustn't he? (*She looks at* LEOPOLD. *The bell of a great church.*)

It is precisely in the hinge between the independence of moral will, claimed and performed, and the crushing imperatives of public order and its necessary pieties, that a drama of moral speculation discovers its resources, and fractures the repression of experience that characterizes a culture industry such as we enjoy, bent on extinguishing pain in a welter of comedy and the inflation of domestic routine into seamless narratives. If it is true, as Adorno suggested, that no great art is ever socially desired, its corollary must be that the desired is an art that contributes only to the restatement of the given. In a series of ten plays called *The Possibilities* that were performed for the first time at the Almeida Theatre in 1986, I attempted to write a set of short narratives that could not be claimed by the audience on the usual territory of moral accord. These included the story of a peasant who would not abandon serfdom even when freedom was forced upon him by his master, a bookseller who believed books were too precious to be wasted on the public, and, in the particular one that follows, a torturer who is possessed of rather more sensibilities than his victims. He arrives in search of lodgings at the house of a woman who has herself been the victim of torture and, as a consequence, has lost the power of speech.

A widow's house. A MAN *arrives with a bag of tools.* THE WOMAN *is seated.*

THE TORTURER. They said if I came here you would have a room. Have you a room? (*She looks at him.*) You have a room? You have a room but you don't know if you like me? Understandable. I am not local and the accent's odd. Perhaps I'm dirty from the road? I'll pay in advance. Or rather, as I have no money yet, I will give you the toolbag as a pledge.

(*He puts the bag down.*) They say they pay on Fridays. What do you say? I am a foreigner, but though I am in many ways unlike you, in others I am identical, so we might progress from there. (*She just looks.*) I don't know what your silence means. I have come across many silent people, but in the end, they spoke. Perhaps that is how it will be with you. I am a skilled man and eat a light breakfast. Also, I sleep soundly and bring no friends back to my lodgings. I am not solitary, but neither am I convivial. What do you say? I won't plead for a room. I would rather lie in a ditch than plead. I am proud, which is perhaps my single fault. (*Pause. He picks up the bag.*) All right, I haven't satisfied you. (*He starts to go, then stops.*) Ah, now I remember. You are deaf and dumb! They told me at the castle, she lets rooms but she is deaf and dumb. Now I have made us both feel foolish! (*He laughs. Pause.*) I am the torturer from Poland and I have been offered a post at the castle. The new lord said there could be no more torture it was against his conscience and dismissed the old one, who, like me, set off across the country in search of a new post. But after six months, the necessity for torture made itself apparent, as it always does, and execution also could not be done without for long, so it was my luck to knock at his gate when the vacancy existed and the need was obvious to all. I have references from previous employers, all of whom were sorry to see me go, but I am a wanderer. I love to travel and I know my trade is never low for long, now shall I go up you unpleasant hag I detest the sight of you and one interview in a day is quite enough. Your eye is fixed on mine like a crow on dying vermin and I know your rooms all stink.

The woman's son, whilst pretending to admire the lodger, plans to murder him in revenge for the agony she has endured, but the torturer is quicker, kills the son, and replaces him in the affections of the mother. The unpredictability of these relationships, and the removal of the elements of moral sympathy that normally dictate the shape of a narrative, made these plays both difficult and fascinating for the audience. A profound resentment at the failure of the evening to deliver affirmations of the familiar kind was coupled with a peculiar will to see it through, a sense of endurance not blandished by platitudes of the 'changed perceptions' variety. It was difficult, and insoluble. It was not a puzzle, however, the satisfactions of it were not cerebral. It was emotional, and it displaced meaning from the confines of the narrow language of 'author's objectives' back to the audience itself. Individuals in the audience could not complain of being cheated, since the terms of the artistic bargain were fulfilled in every respect – the plays were complete in themselves, the characters achieved full autonomy, but somewhere, a convention had been levered out of place, leaving a sense of absence, such as one crossing an arch would balk at the missing keystone. This keystone was moral accord.

A similar impossibility in the architecture of a play characterizes the ruthless pursuit of Helen of Troy in my very much longer play, *The Bite of the Night*, given by the Royal Shakespeare Company at the Pit in 1988. At five hours long, this was deemed such an affront to human tolerance that the RSC box office were given instructions to dissuade potential customers by prefacing all ticket sales with details of its length and obscenity. Some nevertheless found the courage to defy this health warning and expose themselves to what was, if nothing else, a *tour de force* of sustained acting invention by Nigel Terry, about whose extraordinary performance I have written at length elsewhere (pp. 63–64). The narrative is disrupted by the inclusion of act-prologues (pp. 40–44) and scenes of digression, stage poems whose relation to the main action is – a Stanislavskian nightmare – at best peripheral. On top of this, the play moves between times. Thus, the protagonist's academic fascination with Helen of Troy – he is the last classics teacher at a defunct university somewhere in England – is made practical by a series of appalling acts of impiety which, taken together, serve to liberate him and his student into the classical world at the point where Troy has fallen and Helen, restored to her husband, begins her terrible descent. Helen is made the collective's scapegoat for the failure of the eleven societies that are erected on Troy's ruins, but it is Dr Savage, Ph.D., who is the evil genius for all her suffering, the inventor of all her punishments, and the eventual undertaker of her few remains. However, as I explained above, his licence originates in the scattering and destruction of his own family – that contemporary totem – which he achieves in a single afternoon, by a series of inspirations. His child he hands over to a sinister visitor, and his father – the Anchises of the piece – he persuades to commit suicide by suggesting he has been a burden on his own creativity. In other words, it is playing love *against* the family bond that persuades the old man to do away with himself. The vistas of repression that lie behind the debts of family love make this scene simultaneously fascinating and repulsive and set the play off in a condition of *moral suspension* that gives the audience a necessary indication of what is to come. In this scene Dr Savage, watching his weeping child part from him for the last time in the hand of a stranger, sees his chance to disburden himself

[101]

of the old man too. The old man, loyal to the end, is carrying Savage's dinner on a plate. He watches the child depart, a small bag with flannel and toothbrush in his hand. He assumes he is off to a sporting event.

OLD MAN. Football, is it? (*He puts the plate down, starts to go.*)

SAVAGE. I owe you nothing, do I? (*He stops.*) Because you grated on my mother, what's the debt?

OLD MAN. No debt, son.

SAVAGE. And because one not-so-very-mad night I squirmed against his mother, to the ticking of the wedding present and the clatter of the drunkards in the sick-swamped street, so setting in motion the torture of paternity, **I owe no debt, me neither, do I?** (*Pause.*) Argue. Argue for your rights to me.

OLD MAN. No rights.

SAVAGE. No rights . . . (THE OLD MAN *turns to leave again.*) And what is intimacy anyway?

OLD MAN. Search me . . .

SAVAGE. I clung to her and it was two pebbles clashing. (THE OLD MAN *looks.*) When I was in her, hard against her womb, some razor slashed my head, some miniature blade designed to kill conception **you don't expect to find knives in there of all places.** Anyway, it failed, and he was born . . .

OLD MAN (*nodding after* THE BOY). Football today, is it? (*A hiatus of pity.*) Did I ever thank you for the books?

SAVAGE. Books?

OLD MAN. On Homeric Metre. By Dr Savage of the University. To My Father on that great big empty page.

SAVAGE. Christ knows why I –

OLD MAN. An Introduction to the Iliad. In Memory of My Mother.

SAVAGE. Barmy reflex of a clever son –

OLD MAN. No, I –

SAVAGE. **Don't lick feeling off that line of arid print.** (*Pause.*)

OLD MAN. Wha'? (*Pause.*)

SAVAGE. The binding was so poor the leaves fell out. As if they were ashamed to hang with such a dedication –

OLD MAN. Wha'?

SAVAGE. **The sentimental liar I have been.**

OLD MAN. Kind thought I thought . . .

SAVAGE. Kind thought? I hated you. Your mundane opinions. Your repetition of half-truths. Straddling my back. You burden. You dead weight. **He's gone so why don't you.** (THE OLD MAN *turns.*) No one is here for long. Who knows, some death might be already on me. Some growth in the dark, deep wet. Give us some time for my own needs.

[102]

Old bones. Old pelt. (THE OLD MAN *withdraws some yards behind* SAVAGE, *and sits.*) We can have knowledge, but not in passivity. Knowledge exists, but the path is strewn with obstacles. (THE OLD MAN *breaks the plate.*) These obstacles we ourselves erect. (*He takes a shard.*) The conspiracy of the ignorant against the visionary can be broken only by the ruthless intellect. (*He undoes his vest.*) Pity also is a regime. (*He attempts to cut his throat.*) And consideration a manacle.

OLD MAN. Trying . . .

SAVAGE. Manners –

OLD MAN. Trying . . .

SAVAGE. Loyalty –

OLD MAN. Trying, fuck it –

SAVAGE. Responsibility, **iron bands on the brain.** (HOGBIN *enters with a book.*)

HOGBIN. Helen was a whore in any case, it says – (*He sees* THE OLD MAN.) Oi.

SAVAGE. **Knowledge is beyond kindness you know –**

HOGBIN. **Oi!**

SAVAGE. Shut up . . . (THE OLD MAN *succeeds, gurgles.*)

HOGBIN. Hey! Fucking hey!

SAVAGE. I know. I know he is. (HOGBIN *stares at him.* THE OLD MAN *dies.* SAVAGE *suddenly seizes* HOBGIN, *in a horrified embrace.*) **Kiss me, then! My triumph! Kiss me, then!** . . . The death of my father necessitates the cancellation of our next tutorial.

It is in the ambiguities surrounding unforgivable behaviour – moral speculation at its least repentant – that tragedy claims its victims, for to some extent the audience for tragedy *are* victims – of their own curiosity. There is even, perhaps, a price to be paid for such witness, as for the inventor of it. When culture conspires against experience – in the best interests of harmony, perhaps – theatre's special facilities for imaginative discursiveness, its ability to dispense with the disciplines of reality, its self-sufficiency with invented languages, become vital resources for the protection of the private, the unregulated, the disassociated. In such a theatre, the potential for uncoupling the individual from a morally hygienic culture is obvious and threatening. Judgement is suspended, and *debate* – the end of so much dramatic enterprise – redundant. Tragedy's engagement with the forbidden denies the collective its rights over the material of drama; and its innate denial of the domination of deterministic, circumstantial factors in the life of an individual makes it anathema to the ideologists, leading, in Brecht's case, to the groundless accusation that as an art form tragedy belonged only to the dark age of Greek despotism, when in fact the Athenian audience was more practised in democracy than Brecht's own contemporaries. It is the horror of autonomy that bans contemporary tragedy – a horror of an art without claims to the truth, for truth in a humanist theatre is essentially verifiable, either by common experience (the idea of 'recognition' in drama) or by reference to researched material, the 'exposé' being the typical contemporary product of the humanist project. Truth in tragedy is not verifiable, and – in a theatre of moral speculation, banished to that area which the individual, in his solitude, affirms or denies purely by his relation to the actor – it is the performance which turns the audience from potential critics into collaborators and accomplices in an illicit act.

In a recent play – yet to be performed or, perhaps, given its great length, never to be performed – the central narrative is reduced further in scope than in any other play I have attempted, and the effects are designed to be achieved cumulatively by apparently unrelated digressions, rather than through the normal apparatus of story-telling. The play contains four speculations on the story of Abraham and Isaac, in which God, sheltering behind the identity of a vagrant called Benz, quotes the celebrated biblical lines in a number of different contexts. This is the second of the Abrahams. The old man, who is intent on committing a murder as an act of faith, addresses his son, who is apprehensive.

Abraham holding a knife. Isaac enters, stops.

ABRAHAM. I love you. And because I love you, I should not hurt you. It is, after all, a definition of love. (*Pause*). But not the only one. (*Pause*.)

ISAAC. Why is there a fire burning?

ABRAHAM. Another definition might be this. That love conceals nothing. That love is absolute in truthfulness.

ISAAC. And the knife, what's that for?

ABRAHAM. This truthfulness would include the fact of the wholly random nature of existence, which neither pities nor consoles. It is not love to conceal this. It is not love to plaster madness with the fiction of justice or rewards.

ISAAC. I can't stay long because my friend and I –

ABRAHAM. **A new love I have wrung from the very bottom of my life.**

(*Isaac stares*)

ISAAC. Are you going to the city for a . . . (*Pause*.) But never mind . . . (*Pause*.)

[104]

ABRAHAM. I felt, once I felt, oh, so shallowly, Isaac, that you would live, and marry, and inherit, and enjoy, and see, and own, and exercise good judgement – judgement partly learned from me – measure, criticise, and sometimes, complain. (*Pause.*) A fallacy permitted to all parents **But I honour you with deeper truths my son.** (*Pause.*) I tell you, rather, the savage and relentless nature of all life. (*Pause.*) What other parent would? What other parent cast aside the consoling lies of parenthood? **None I promise you.** Kiss me!

(*Isaac goes to him, and kisses him.*)

To share in this, to wade in this, absurdity, demeans the very soul.

ISAAC. I never heard you speak like this before and why the fire, it's hot today?

ABRAHAM. Always I smothered the evidence. In song-singing. In dance-dancing. In love-acting. And why? **That you likewise should be deceived?** No, this chain of deception must be snapped. And you – you are the link.

(*Pause. Benz enters, watches casually. Isaac perceives the drift and makes to escape, but Abraham has him by the waist.*)

This also is a love!

(*He floors Isaac and holds the knife prepared. Benz speaks.*)

BENZ. A ram is caught by its horns.

(*Pause.*)

ABRAHAM. What . . . ?

BENZ. Just there. Sacrifice the ram instead.

(*A terrible pause. Abraham releases his grip on Isaac, who rises to his feet.*)

ISAAC. Are you ill? Come to the house. You're ill.

(*Abraham sways, Isaac looks at Benz, and runs away. Pause.*)

ABRAHAM. Why?

BENZ. No reason.

ABRAHAM. Why?

BENZ. No reason at all.

ABRAHAM. **I have unpicked my brain for this!** (*He looks at Benz, painfully.*) How else could I assent?

BENZ. You cheated me.

ABRAHAM. Cheated . . . ?

BENZ. What sacrifice was it, when you convinced yourself that life was vile? It was a liberation you were threatening your loved boy with . . .

(*Pause.*)

ABRAHAM. Forgive me, I do not understand what –

BENZ. Oh, they all say that!

(*Abraham stares at the ground.*)

You were to submit, in all clarity, in the fullness of understanding, to the wholly irrational act. You were to kill your son without the benefit of philosophy. You were to make no sense of the deed, but to endure the purest pain. For my sake.

ABRAHAM. Why . . .

(*Pause.*)

BENZ. No reason. No reason at all . . .

(*Pause. Suddenly Abraham launches himself at Benz and tries to strangle him. They stagger in an embrace. There is a cry off, from Isaac. He rushes in, seizes the knife, and plunges it into Benz, who falls. Abraham looks at the dead figure on the floor.*)

ABRAHAM. Oh, now things will be hard . . . Now we will have only ourselves to blame . . .

(*Isaac runs away, ignoring Abraham's call. He runs into a street in Rome.*)

There is, perhaps, nothing which might be characterized as sacrilegious in the liberal climate of contemporary Christianity, and the retelling of myth is a practice as old as art itself. What these imaginary histories are intended to create, however, is a climate of moral uncertainty. In the absence of any satirical structures (and it is worth noticing the continuing authority of satire in establishing moral norms in contemporary theatre) this permits an audience to shed its burden of carefully compiled certainties and expose itself to what is, in effect, the chaos of an experience in which security is absent. All the acquired habits of public performance militate in favour of unity of response and dispensed enlightenment. Far from being a place of moral adventure the theatre has become disciplined by its responsibilities – spurious responsibilities to the collective, to social progress, harmony and so on, which have effectively stifled its ambition and its potential for unpicking conventional wisdom. Theatre is appropriated by the forward march of common decency.

If tragedy is speculation on behaviour, a modern tragedy must entail a painful loneliness, for both the dramatist and the audience, since the old recourse to religion, or the social obligation to punish transgression, is the factor of unification that cannot be recalled – even by reference to the popular will. Only through the obligations of solidarity can the community play – a particular phenomenon of the last decade – make its hollow appeal to civic virtues. For the modern tragedy, division is not only the subject, but the *object* of the artistic enterprise. It is discord that must characterize a theatre in an age of populism, and the theatre company, dramatist and actors alike, must cease to revere themselves as articulators of social scandal, the *lacrimae rerum* of late democracy, or the paralysis of bourgeois life – the deadening inheritance of Chekhovian nostalgia –

and revere themselves as something else – for revere themselves they must, it is no longer an age for workshops and the journeymen who are appropriate to them. When the atmosphere is thick with sentimental homage to welfare and community, the theatre – ever the enemy of order – will speak in discordant tones, it will strike that bargain with impossibility that has characterized its best moments – flagrancy, outrage, permission, a privileged space for madness, and a filter against news.

I would like to conclude with a quotation from my latest play, *Ten Dilemmas in the Life of a God*, which takes as its theme what is perhaps the greatest transgression of all – impotence, in this case a sexual impotence jointly effected by a man and woman whose form of desire – much to the fury of family and village – precludes, abolishes, sexual union, and thereby prohibits the collective's prime function – reproduction of itself. The man, Draper, has been imprisoned for an apparently motiveless murder, but one which has served to keep him from the object of his appalling need. He comes home to the enthusiastic greeting of his sisters, and the suspicious regard of his lover, Paula. He reflects on the experience of gaol:

DRAPER. At one time I thought the whole world lied in unison to hurt me but all the gaoled think that we are so tender we are so bruised and gradually the louts received their letters me however never me never this was certainly a distinction this adamantine silence they pitied me and yet I was not diminished and wore this smile because I knew you loved me or not loved no the louts talked love no I lived in you with or without permission I inhabited your arteries and stalked your brain love no the very word a lout's word surely I thought I had abolished it but I lack consistency in all things but one and that's

(*He stops abruptly. Silence. The dog barks.*)

My (*Pause.*) **Don't let me out I said**

I was not sincere

Don't let me out

Not entirely sincere

Obviously I yearned the fields the meadows the trams etcetera obviously the faces of my sisters and the racing clouds yes those obviously but

Paula to resume with Paula

And they offered me a ticket to another place they do that they name five towns and I did hesitate I thought of their cathedrals yes cathedral towns they were some in the South some in the frontier district I might be sitting on the train now scouring the horizon for the spires to come into view but no I'm here as if I'm here notwithstanding and you know I love cathedrals

Back
Back
As if choices were
Back
A fiction of the inveterately political
(*He gets up, goes to each of his sisters and kisses them on the head.*)
Forgive me
I could have been so much
Oh, what a life I might have
But I exist only to make love to this woman which (*Pause. A distant train climbs an incline.*) I never have yet and . . . (*Pause.*) May never . . .

Recognition as aesthetic paralysis in theatre*

The artistic intention of humanist drama is the presentation of man
in the social context in which he moves and under the psychological
conditions which afflict him. It is a project of representation, a form
of mimesis which goes beyond typicality to particularity and whose
intentions, on the one hand, are socializing, civilizing or revolutionary
for the audience and, on the other, entail a discharge of conscience
for the dramatist.

The essential characteristic of such a form is the notion of truth,
a truth which can be validated only by an act of recognition.
Recognition is the governing principle of the dramatic form which
has dominated European theatre practice since the Enlightenment.
This moment of recognition is simultaneously the igniting spark of
the experience of the play and the certain extinction of imaginative
trespass. Thus the play exists within strict demarcations, and these
demarcations are set by the audience itself which is invited to seek
comparisons with the stage matter from its own experience, validating
it by its 'possibility' or 'probability', and thereby assisting at its own
intellectual and imaginative execution, perhaps a definition of 'entertainment' as a phenomenon. It is flattered with the false entitlement
to judge what it witnesses according to the degree of recognition
achieved by the writer and the actor. How successfully reality is
reproduced, how convincingly the actor imitates, how authentic are
the emotional states generated on the stage, are all self-maiming
critical categories the audience is encouraged to apply.

Each of these judgements, which places the audience in a critical
posture at the outset, is a wilful limitation of the experience of theatre
and a manifestation of fear of the irrational which inundates the
humanist mode; in invoking the concept of recognition humanist
theatre disguises its repressive instinct, disguising it as social responsibility, critical vitality, celebration or the carnivalesque. By making

* Given at the British Council Summer School, London, 7 August 1992.

the success or failure of a dramatic work dependent on the reproduction of experience from *outside* the walls of the theatre, subordinating it to the suffocating principle of *imitation*, humanist artistic theology severs man from his own malevolent nature, his promiscuity of thought.

Theatre might be viewed instead as a de-civilizing experience, a series of permissions to transgress, an act of indiscipline or a mutiny whose forms are inverted reflections of conventional morality or moral speculations given entitlement of expression by virtue of the physical and emotional barriers separating it from the world. A theatre is a privileged space, and a theatre without walls, either literally of the street or one rigidly determined by principles of recognition, is no longer privileged. The wall excludes the State, the police, the priest, but also the activist, the social worker and the revolutionary. A theatre without walls is a theatre that has forfeited its privacy, and privacy in an age of dissemination, access and populism, is authentic rebellion. If the theatre's walls once permitted the indulgence of bourgeois fantasy at the expense of knowledge, they now protect the freedom to imagine from the humanist regime of relevance and collective discipline. In asserting the right to privacy, the non-humanist theatre establishes its cardinal aesthetic – the autonomy of the work of art as staged *and* viewed, the discrepancies and disunities of the audience being as crucial to the experience as the absence of consistency on the stage.

Let me state here unequivocally that theatre is without use, is the abnegation of use–value, and defies annexation or appropriation, being neither a diversion from the tedium of common life nor a palliative for deformed social relations, and therefore it reconciles no one either to his neighbour or his fate. It is more likely to induce rage or melancholy, even a disposition to suicide, than it is to initiate reflective action or rational discrimination. Its nature is torrential, barbaric, non-evidential, its methods are those of plethora and excess, and by its very origin in simulation, theatre is an unlikely host for the ameliorative project of humanism and its hyperbole of truth.

To achieve the eruption of theatre from the repressive aesthetic of recognition requires, as I have indicated, a prima facie assertion of theatre as privileged space, adjacent to but not *of* the social world, but furthermore, the demolition of the portals of delight which are the infantile pleasures of recognition, and their replacement with the sombre doorway of *anxiety*.

Anxiety must be the condition of witnessing drama that takes moral *speculation*, and not social *imitation*, as its unfaltering objective. This tension is the effect of *failing to recognize* an action, a character or a type, an uneasy rocking of all popular cultural modes. In failing to recognize and, consequently, being unable to predict (predictability being a breach of the contract between audience and stage), elements of the unconscious are stimulated which are denied in humanist drama, elements of primitive and pre-social fear, choices of the instinctive and even self-destructive kind, the very sorts of behaviour which constitute the *unrealistic*.

In complete contradistinction to the humanist theatre therefore, the ordering of experience is posterior, and not anterior, to the event witnessed. This ordering of experience is made, it if is made at all, by the audience in its individual, atomized form, and not by the director or by the dramatist applying theories of production, laws of clarity or cramping objectification. The creation of 'sympathetic' characters becomes of less importance than the creation of dynamic ones, because to 'sympathize' is essentially to recognize, to pity, rather than to be implicated oneself. The dynamic character is one who commands attention, whose actions are mesmeric, impulsive and unlicensed, not insane but socially criminal, whose virtues are explorations, and not ratifications, of the normal.

The Unrecognizable Theatre is one of emotion, irrationality and beauty, not of order, discipline, or the collective will as shaped by the contemporary conscience. It licenses behind its walls and in its darkness the privacy of unsupervised emotion, and in the absence of harmony as a pervasive principle, a Utopian repression, it allows the possible to exist as a spectre, both horror and affirmation.

The theatre lies under a shroud

Conscience kills art as surely as pity kills love. This is the miserable condition of our greatest art, where critics, directors and dramatists conspire to instruct us in political responsibility. Brecht (mercifully without conscience) suffered a comprehensible lack of nerve when facing the impotence of drama at the spectacle of a triumphant fascism, and indulged the grossest simplification of complex psychologies for political ends. A less justified cowardice distinguishes the liberal humanists who manage our great theatres now, those honoured with the task of reproducing the national ideology. Any theatre offering further versions of *Arturo Ui* or *The Accidental Death of an Anarchist* perpetuates the old lie of identifying the enemy and leaving the innocent immune – political theatre at its basest. But the innocent do not exist and Brecht's weakest impulse only massages the idealist absurdity that the bad can be told by their uniforms (Police, Capitalists, Vegetable Market Crooks), leaving the audience to relax in the secure knowledge the indictment does not include them . . .

The Political Theatre remains what it always was – what it must be, since politics is the art of simplification – psychologically shallow and a trumpet call to actions no one will perform, a dutiful raising of conscience (if not consciousness) that elevates the dramatist to the preposterous position of The One Who Knows, for while there can be no Geniuses any more (egalitarianism could not tolerate it) and the Author is dead (he/she must be, in case he utters a forbidden thought in terms you cannot forget), the Great Researchers are always among us, telling us the truth on stage ('dramatizing') we are told we cannot discover elsewhere. Thus hierarchy persists, in spite of so much disavowal, because the theatre of Enlightenment requires its teachers, those who will promote the false ideal that the Theatre Changes the World. It never changed the world, of course, but at its best it complicated it, making action even less likely than before. This the Greeks knew long before Socrates, being practitioners of the thing Political Theatre runs headlong from, the thing that filled Brecht with righteous horror – tragedy.

Tragedy, unlike the Theatre of Conscience, requires no validation, nor can it be inspected for documentary faults, its truth or untruth. It asserts nothing in its own defence – not its therapeutic essences, its cathartic effects on social behaviour, nothing Aristotelian at all, and certainly it is anathema to the improvers of the social world, for even where it asserts collective values it can do so only with an ill-disguised bad faith – in a spirit of compromise, with an eye to the church or the State. Tragedy exists simply because the pain of others, and subsequently our own, is a necessity to witness – not to make sense of, not for a utility value, but as something for itself – which is not to say it is Art For Art's Sake, the forbidden, oh, so forbidden secret thing that dare not speak its name – it is Pain For Pain's Sake, and how we as a culture shrink from pain, how all political parties are cemented in the same pursuit and share as their highest slogan 'We Will Eradicate All Pain', how we obscure it, and make the fatuous giggle of comedy the deafening chorus of our age. We can unite on our dislike of pain. Tragedy, however, is the terror of mediocrity and progressive ideologies alike. It is about infringement, and about the Self. It dislocates the conscience, and damages goodwill. In mass society, it has to struggle to exist.

The masses cannot be served. Whilst it is the vanity of the entertainment industry to posture as the allies of the inarticulate, only individuals can be stimulated by a work of art, and only those individuals with *a desire for complication* (nauseous with collective truths and endless access to all things except the experience of tragedy) will find in it the ecstasy of moral uncertainty. The individual who aches to know suffering as an entrance to an unknown world will sit in the dark (crucially dark, to disengage from his neighbours) and watch theatre's unforgotten (though lying beneath a shroud of conscience) pact with illegitimacy. In contrast to the humanist play, or the socialist play, the Play of Conscience in its many forms, the tragedy demands you leave your morals at the door, for in this space (absolutely not the street, but privileged) the beauty of the actor is not blurred by urges to *educate, elucidate or edify* – the message is absent, the message is abolished by *obscurity* (in an age obsessed with 'accessibility' what greater crime could the artist and the actor commit?)

[113]

Oh Michael, Poor Michael,
Who thinks Art civilizes you . . .

In mass society, great art is never socially desired, for it declines
the offer of instant gratification, it defies the ordinance to entertain,
and repudiates the collective will. Modern tragedy, which I have
elsewhere described as Catastrophist, sins against the suffocating
burden of the Brechtian and Stanislavskian method, with their
narrowly conceived objectives and repressive pursuits of clarities. It
celebrates the complexity of motivation, it enhances contradiction
and extols *the beauty of language* against the naturalistic, populist and
mechanistic metres of the street. It proclaims the theatre as the
natural resort of poetry and therefore insists on a new acting. The
political dramatist is above all concerned with the narrow goal of
communication – the tragic dramatist with *complication*; the political
dramatist begins from the assumption that the audience shares
beliefs, the tragic dramatist from the desire to break the solidarity of
his audience into atoms.

The Theatre of Conscience paralysed the actor (he or she could
not be permitted to divert attention by his personality from the issue
under *debate*) and subsequently paralysed the audience, which became
under the Brecht/Stanislavsky/Royal Court schools seized by *critical
attitudes* – it found a way of witnessing theatre which endowed it with
false entitlements to *judge the material* (in the political play, the
argument must be presented) instead of experiencing the emotions.
It came to the theatre trained with critical impulses and anxious lest
the meaning could not be instantly induced – the enlightened
approving the approvable, fatigued by conventional truths, awash
with yet more pity for what it had already learned to pity, its
sympathies fixed in advance, wearily expectant (yet fearful for its
absence) of *yet another humanist platitude*. This was surely one of
theatre's poorest passages, when so much of its store of powers was
contemptuously consigned to *the aesthetic*, as if this category
were suspect, reactionary and decadent, when in reality it was the
journalistic impulse in threatre that had made it truly decadent.

Oh, Michael, Poor Michael,
Who thinks Art tells the truth . . .

The journalist had defeated the poet, but not for long, since the
instincts of theatre revolted against the endless *dramatizing of events*,

and in any case it could not compete with the swift technology of the entertainment industry. The great consensus of *anti-pain* dealt the Political Theatre so many blows, not least the blow of being itself *socially correct*, part and parcel of the great collective conscience (*Miss Saigon, Les Misérables*, impeccably conscience-stricken and humanist). The theatre, uneasy under the shroud, reaches for its banished powers – *pain, poetry, and the actor's voice* – and the audience, yet to be born, but stirring in its discontent, longs to locate there what it cannot find elsewhere, for theatre must be an experience distinct from other forms and not reproducible there. It must discover in chaos and in pain the substance of social disorder, for the irony of art was always this, that it lent power to the powerless by its embracing of the forbidden, not by its reiteration of collective norms. *Theatre for what, therefore? For nothing*, for no end, and for the silencing of all those dramatists who routinely declare, as if their art required justification, 'I wanted people to know . . . such and such . . .', 'I wanted people to understand each other better . . .', a modesty which hardly conceals the arrogance of the self-appointed enlightener. It is, like all great arts, for itself alone, and the tragedy is written because it cannot tolerate the strain of silence any more.

The state of loss as the end of a dramatic performance

The theatre of humanism, radical criticism and celebration seeks a single end, the reassurance of the audience, the satisfaction of the bargain struck at the box office between the purchasers of comfort and the suppliers of delight. The payment entails a dispensation from the actors to the audience in the form of *perceptions*. This is the gratification of expectations, the sordid currency of spiritual exchange, inevitably barren. I left with more than I brought in. My store was enhanced. I profited.

In the Theatre of Catastrophe the foyer has none of the hum which characterizes the stock exchange of entertainment. The end of the efforts of writer, director, actors, is a *state of loss*. Nothing is described here by the term *creative*, the discredited alibi of populist culture in search of a leisure which is ethically justified. The *State of Loss* describes a state of lost morality, an ethical vacuum, a denial, a rebuke to order, a melancholy and a pain. It is a revelation of the essential terror of the world, and an abyss. The ability of an audience to expose itself to these absences is possible only through the heroic efforts of the actor and the unflinching qualities of the text. Only by poetry can melancholy be made tolerable, and only the poetic actor can bear the audience through its pain. This pain is *necessity*. The Theatre of Catastrophe is not the comfort of a cruel world, but the cruelty of the world made manifest and found to be – *beautiful*.

Two Bradshaws*

Covington was strung in the quickness of her nerves, already dislocated at the opening. In her the revolt against Utopia was already running and discipline alone had maintained a ménage of political responsibility. Thus the fall of the theorists, like the fall of a forest, allowed a blaze of light into an overshadowed soul. In Kelly, duty and collaboration were beaten out of her, as the brain of a boxer is loosened by his bouts, first by horror, then by abuse.

Covington was wit by instinct, a thing hidden from a humourless husband, a private and treasured resource. Kelly invented wit from the spectacle of horror, a thing to shield her eyes. In these different actresses, the terror of Utopia was varyingly described, its eating of the instincts, its fastening on fear. For Bradshaw-the-man was the supreme intelligence of idealism, the compendium of arguments whose patient expositions are the silent score to every action of the play, the intolerable presence of the harmonious achieved by force and reason, abolition, exhortation and the ban. From this avalanche of theory Bradshaw-the-woman flees with an inspired shame – Covington taking her revenge with every sarcasm in a spirit of youth previously denied, Kelly less adolescent, the rupturing of a partnership wounding more and the shock to reason reverberating in a scarce-believing soul. Covington sang with a liberated temper, some beating of wings never unfolded. Kelly, unloaded, disassembling a life and a household, with all this onerous word implies. She had been a collaborator, so that her freedom was wrung only from strenuous will. Covington could only have been the victim of a genius's gaze, and consequently flourished on the roads as if vagrancy were natural to her. In both, the reassembling of the man was the pretext for his abolition, the breaking with a past whose lingering inspirations generated nothing in them but a ferocious pity smothered

* Julie Covington, The Joint Stock Company, 1983. Tricia Kelly, The Wrestling School, 1991. Bradshaw is the protagonist of *Victory*.

[117]

with contempt – an ecstasy of cruelty necessarily poured on the head of a lipless acolyte.

In both Kelly and Covington, a power of emotional truth alone could substitute for the text's refusal of staged 'developments', the method of exposition by motivation, sympathy or objective. Since the text forbade the familiar deceit of allowing the audience to feel 'they would do the same' under the circumstances, insisting instead on impossible circumstances and unpredictable events, Kelly and Covington plunged those reservoirs of feeling which the liberal/ Utopian theatre bans – as Bradshaw-the-man banned the incomprehensible from his Harmonia, making sex an anaesthetized androgyny which even Scrope finds inadequate to experience. In these inspiring performances, the will-to-life, which forever entails the undoing of conventional truth, was therefore primarily an internal excavation of illicit feeling which in its purity and cruelty possesses the beauty of all incompatible things; Utopia abhors the incompatible, which is the source of its inevitable staleness and savagery.

The idea of promiscuity in the Theatre of Catastrophe*

The Critical Theatre, which for the sake of argument I shall take to be that of Brecht, Shaw and the bulk of our contemporaries, is essentially a theatre of clear objectives. It is predicated on the idea of 'saying'. In the Critical Theatre the play 'says' something to the audience, and the elucidation of this 'saying' is the function of the production, the aim of the director and actors alike. The contemporary audience is now thoroughly versed in this method, and a party to it, by training and experience. So much so, in fact, that it brings with it the demand that the play should 'say' unambiguously – a demand which, if unsatisfied, leaves this audience with the nagging sense that the dramatist and the actors are guilty of an act of collective bad faith. Consequently, the Critical Theatre moves inexorably towards an art of anodyne humanism, in which the actors and the audience tacitly collaborate in an act of 'saying' and the theatre diminishes itself in pursuit of the limited objective of communicating an idea, albeit in the form of a narrative. Behind this lies the notion of the author as a 'good' man or woman, whose trade is principally the dispensing of wisdom and whose vocation is the creation of harmony.

In this collective deception, where the audience is traditionally ranked above the stage like benches of judges for receiving and validating the idea, and where clarity becomes a fetish, falsely democratic in its elimination of ambiguity, what the play 'says' becomes merely the pretext for debate – the play is a means, not an end. What occurs therefore, when the play says nothing? What chaos ensues when the text refuses to admit an objective and evades clarity? What nightmare awaits an audience when the time-honoured Brechtian/Stanislavskian contract is denied, the contract which has as its main clause the obligation to communicate the idea? This is breakdown, of course, in the essentially polite social relations of the contemporary theatre, leading to a suspicion that the dramatist has no

* Given as a paper at the University of Exeter, 10 May 1991.

morals and the actors are being misused. Under these circumstances, the theatre becomes not a locus for the restatement of collectively-approved positions – hostility to war, hatred of exploitation, the rights of women – not a place in other words, for the rehearsal of humanist platitudes – but a site, or a landscape, for a morally promiscuous journey in which – since there is no objective – the detours are likely to be as significant as the route itself. The single most important consequence of such a mutiny against governing principles is the overthrow of the audience.

The notion of the audience as an indivisible authority with rights of judgement over works of imagination is central to the Critical Theatre, but it is an authority only so long as the dramatist regards himself as tutor, enlightener, truth-teller. If he or she refuses to plead an argument, and offers instead the spectacle of a free imagination disciplined not by morality but by an aesthetic of language and vision the audience is obliged to approach the work with neither power nor contempt – it is not under these circumstances anything strictly 'truthful' that is on show, there is no criterion from politics or consensus against which it can be judged. The net effect of this is that the stage acquires an authority over the audience, and in symbolic space this would entail the audience sitting on an inferior plane to the actor, who is no longer the didactic agent of clarity but something dangerously unreliable, something altogether more hypnotic and unlicensed. This is a theatre which abolishes debate, in which the play is a substitute for debate, and without obligation to notions of entertainment or enlightenment, neither 'delightful' nor instructive, it resolves nothing – on the contrary, resolution is anathema: it is tragedy without catharsis, tragedy in which the audience is implicated in the acts of cruelty it witnesses, and from which there is no relief or refuge in the reiteration of the utilitarian concept of the public good. It is, consequently, a theatre of silence and contemplation.

Given that dissension in mass society is almost an obligation, a theatre of promiscuity requires no special justification – indeed to talk of art requiring justification at all is one of the melancholy consequences of humanist culture – but its particular interest lies in its refutation of the *solution* as a moral category, for just as the Critical Theatre *says* the *idea*, it implies necessarily the idea of the *solution*, which is, broadly speaking, the elimination of pain as the universal objective of human effort. The humanist theatre, along with its

Marxist and Christian allies, poses painlessness, the elimination of tensions, as ideals against which the drama is judged; conflict exists only to be resolved. Art does not simply exist – it is annexed as part of the armoury in the struggle for human perfection. The narrating of facts in the researched play, the description of conflict or poverty of communication in the domestic play, the retailing of injustices in the play of issues, comedies of misunderstandings, are all essentially demonstrations of the possibility of the Solution for which the audience hankers, and which it pathetically believes it can discover in the mind of the dramatist. It seems to me there is a profound sadness in the relationship between the Reconciler – the dramatist – and the Seekers after Harmony – the audience – in the humanist theatre, a Utopian pathos which affects both Chekhov's appalling gift for renunciation and Brecht's hammering insistence that we can discover the Truth if we look hard enough. Even an idea as seemingly innocuous as Harmony hides within it the shadow of the torture chamber.

If the Theatre of Catastrophe willingly divests the dramatist of his divine status as dispenser of truth or harmony, and the audience of its absurd status as monolithic critic, what is it that constitutes the substance of the transaction between them? What is the theatre that has no Saying? Its method can only be the erosion of narrative, because narrative is itself the first element in the construction of moral meaning. What occurs in the form of consecutive scenes, or in real time played on the stage, inevitably implies a moral perspective unless the seductive effect of the stage is subverted, as I attempted in *Victory* – a highly narrative play but one in which intense imaginative efforts are made – by me in the first instance – to prevent the audience wandering into a state of dreamy sympathy with a preordained morality, the sort of Christian–humanist ethic that says all victims are good. Susan Bradshaw is relentlessly bad, even if she is a victim of political pendulums.

In later works of Catastrophic Theatre, I have attempted to deny narrative its authority by resorting to digression – certainly in *The Bite of the Night*, where time itself is also dethroned from its eminence, and in my most recent play, *Rome*, where the existence of one narrative is continually displaced by the eruption of others which only tangentially relate to it in terms of theme. I might also mention in this regard *The Last Supper*, the first play of The Wrestling School, which parallels one familiar narrative with parables of a completely amoral, and possibly incomprehensible, nature – or indeed, *The Possibilities*, ten related plays, which are simply scenes, on the theme of making terrible but necessary mistakes, the very idea of the Necessary Mistake being wholly inappropriate to the Theatre of Saying or a Theatre of Solutions. Apart from this disruption of narrative discipline, a second means of dislocation – and dislocation is the function of art in a time of smothering consensus – is the employment of the Chorus, which stands outside, and interferes with, the working of the Realist narrative, often in a form which refuses the audience the opportunity to take its statements for granted – I am thinking here of the wholly unreliable chorus in *Golgo* – but which also permits the restoration of poetry to the stage, thereby insisting on the distinction between the stage and common life. If the humanist theatre is essentially unpoetic, because it can only assert the collective language, the Catastrophic Theatre insists on the distinction between stage and street, and on the peculiarities of the dramatist's voice; it will not renounce its licence to speculate both on how things are done, and also on how things are said.

The question so often raised about all forms of artistic practice – 'how does this help us?', the anxious cry of the alienated in mass society – is best countered by refuting its very formulation, which threatens to diminish art and to render it as utilitarian as any other kind of manufacture. The Catastrophic Theatre cannot satisfy this mechanistic demand because its ecstatic possibility lies in its denial of the possibility of Solution. As a form of theatre it is so overloaded, so apparently excessive in language, metaphor, event, diversity of form and image, so promiscuous in its speculation, it denies the very concept of the ordered life even as an ideal. It is a non-Utopian art which pits cruelty against pity and recognizes their coexistence in the guilty and the innocent alike. Who could take sides when the court of Charles II exposes the spectacle of Scrope, maimed, in a wedding cake? The merciless humour of Charles II draws the audience into a conspiracy of his wit rather than into indignation at the fate of a decent man. It is indeed difficult to state whether any character in a Catastrophic play commits a bad act, so complex is the state of emotion which surrounds it. I have often said that the audience for this kind of theatre needs to re-fashion itself, since what it brings from conventional theatre merely excludes it from the experience – there needs to be a surrender of the critical habit, the value-assessment of the Brechtian school, the posture of offence, and, instead, a wilful abnegation of loyalties. So much contemporary theatre consists of the statement of loyalties, to gender, to ideology, to concepts of the progressive, even to melancholy, whilst the Catastrophic Theatre replaces loyalty with an aesthetic of will to experience – it discovers light in the unlikeliest places and air where it seemed at first impossible to breathe. It is my contention that the twin disciplines of entertainment and enlightenment have relegated theatre to a position of philosophical impotence, and that its much-vaunted ability to 'respond' to issues, its journalistic flirtations with research, have merely rendered it down to a classifiable commodity, a suitable product for the morality of a national theatre. In a promiscuous theatre, nothing is given or predicated, neither rebellion nor abnegation, and its aims are not to console but to stimulate a restlessness which is not – as in the classic tragic formula – discharged, but carried away by the individuals of the audience whose contrasting reactions to what they have witnessed divides them against themselves. I repeat that no one is educated by a play of this sort – no information, useful or otherwise, is communicated, nor is communication the essence. The actor is elevated, through language and through the extent of the pain he embodies, to a dominant status, one which obviates pity or judgement. The effect of this is that debate – the stimulation of which is the purpose of the Critical play – is abolished, the grounds for it subsumed *in* the production, rather than the production providing dramatized material to stimulate argument. The promiscuity of the imagination in the Catastrophic play, its unapologetic intimacy with the forbidden – indeed, the rupturing of the forbidden as a category – evacuates the territory of values. The production must become, in essence, a poem, and, like a poem, not reducible to a series of statements in other forms. In these terms, the experience of pain, which is the most significant emotion, is not viewed as a subject for amelioration, or abolition, nor made material for a moral argument, a pretext for Utopian aspirations, but is affirmed in itself, and for itself. The liberating of pain from its social subjects, and from its so-called objective conditions, is possible only in a theatre which is essentially promiscuous in moral terms, and, far from becoming what is inevitably described as 'pessimistic', affirms the individual's right to chaos, extremity and self-description.

On the sickness of the audience*

I talked about the sickness of the audience
The democratic indignation!
The froth of injured innocence!
One even threatened suicide if theatre did not save
The world
As if the people could be wrong!
And this cascade of passionate rebukes
Such as
Only a bad workman blames his tools
But who said the audience were tools?
They witness
That is their privilege
No
It's obvious an audience can be sick
If democracies can be
Mobs often are
It's time perhaps for artists to get off their knees
Audiences learn bad habits
Viruses affect them in their nerves
And maim their sensibilities
Wherever crowds assemble infections spread
Especially from critics
Those coughing celebration who are perhaps already dead
No you shouldn't come too near to these
And theatre managers with or without beliefs
From the access-mad and the I-have-my-rights bacillus
A soul might take a chill
And obviously from dramatists an audience might get ill
I spare no one
Certainly the sickness does exist
The symptoms can be annotated
The myopia of thinking all things must be clear

* The Birmingham University Theatre Conference, 1991.

The tumescence caused by the appetite for enlightenment
The unhealthy craving for laughter
The morbid horror of taking offence
The apoplexy of having paid good money to see this
The feverish ache for moral platitudes
The incoherent belief in the weakness of man
The low temperature requiring massage of existing beliefs
The proneness to falling into states of pity for others
The greater proneness to pitying themselves
The seizure of the muscles at the sight of pain
It is a list
Certainly it is now proper to declare
The audience requires a change of air

Eleven building bricks

1

The actor is a liar who must be credited. That much is obvious. But his lies cannot be modest. Who requires a modest liar? We go to be properly deceived.

2

The actor is a liar on our behalf. In the lies of the stage we punish the liars of life.

3

The theatre makes us ashamed of our sensitivities. Their shallowness. Their narrowness. The theatre mocks the dominating passion of our lives – self-preservation. In life we say always 'Thus far and no further, my sanity demands it . . .' In the theatre we say 'Thus far and further still, my sanity demands it . . .'

4

How weak it is to hear an audience was 'moved'. And even weaker to hear how it was 'informed'. Better that the audience was enraged, not from the antics of offence, but from the exposure of its hidden crimes. These crimes – the worst crimes – are crimes against personal experience. Theatre indicts the unlived life.

5

It was fear of theatre that made them drag it back into the street. They saw the crowd would smother it, as it aches to smother all seducers.

6

The audience asks to escape. But escape to where? Over the wall is another wall. It is probably no use to know this. The theatre's knowledge is not of the useful kind, however.

7

The theatre teaches nothing. Sometimes however, there is a plethora of teachers. It is better then to go to a dreamer, and if she misleads you, so what? You are misled. What is love, but to be misled from oneself?

8

'I did not understand the play.' 'You were not invited to understand it. We did not understand it, either. We merely believed it. Do you want to diminish all life?'

9

It was beautiful, but not in any way I already understood the beautiful. This particular beauty came in the guise of the ugly.

10

Theatre draws apart. It draws the audience away from its beliefs. It draws the social from the individual. It draws the individual from himself. At the exit doors, the audience finds it hard to sew its life together again. Some of this audience secretly hopes it cannot be drawn together again . . .

11

'Who wrote the play?' 'What was he saying?' Why must you seek to know his saying? It is the shape of his effort that constitutes the art.

Stages in the education of an audience

The resistance of the audience to what it witnesses works in our favour given

> the numb state of society
>
> the circulation of conventional wisdom
>
> the dearth of serious criticism

The audience comes to the new reluctantly and at differing speeds

It is unconsoled by a theatre of tragedy but learns to forgo consolation given

> society's obsession with comfort
>
> the political obsession with the elimination of pain
>
> the popular pursuit of pleasure

It begins to demand further exposure to the formerly unpalatable and in so doing

Recognizes theatre as the *solitary* source for spiritual pain since the refusal of pain diminishes the soul and this is *recognized* . . .

The relations between an affronted audience and the actor

AUDIENCE
Expectations → Unfulfilled → Alienation

THE ACTOR
The Cynosure

→ Suspension → Rapture → Silence → Loss

THE ACTOR
Beauty

The anatomy of a sob*

For fifteen years I had watched McDiarmid's engagement with my texts.

That Good Between Us. The Love of a Good Man. Crimes in Hot Countries. Downchild. The Castle. Pity in History. The Early Hours of a Reviled Man.

He had given extraordinary performances unique in the theatre.

He had created a style.

He had married the body to the voice.

He explored the unforgivable.

He excavated the illegal.

He tortured himself.

He was unrepentant.

He brought the private to the public.

He would not tolerate indifference.

He was shameless and therefore mythical.

After these fifteen years he played another text, *Terrible Mouth*. In this, he was deaf, sick, voyeuristic, self-hating, self-advertising, sexually mad, tortured, pitiless, adoring. It was a role created for him, who loves the extremes. In this opera, he was required to sob. This sob he treated as part of the text and not a thing incidental to it. In it he saw not a momentary loss of articulation, but an opportunity. Always he seized the opportunity for other means of articulation – the seizure of an object, a garment, the annexation of things was part of his way as an actor. Here he found in the sob not a conclusion to an emotion, but the essence of it, and therefore

---

* *Terrible Mouth*, the opera by Nigel Osborne, libretto by Howard Barker, the Almeida Theatre, 1992.

brought to it that same excoriation and invention that attended on every line he spoke. He invested it with his physical resources as well as his mental agony so that his body struggled with the failure of words, as if words had been driven out of the cavities they inhabited – lungs, mouth, and arching throat – leaving gasping muscularity behind them, and into this vacuum flooded nothing but incomprehensible pain. The loss of language was like the loss of oxygen to a diver. Without speech his body writhed in dumb agony, desperate to articulate but betrayed by articulation, and in this silence he began to drown, for speech, as long as it existed, enabled him to thrash the waves of self-contempt and loneliness that plunged over him, but, speechless, he swiftly succumbed, a wreckage of jaw and tilted cave of mouth. He hung here as the unwillingly delivered sound of moral capitulation gathered from every extremity of his body, the sob which, overwhelming his reluctance, uttered itself into a silence of seized time. This sound was unearthly, recognizable only from the smothered pains of too-private life, or appalling memories of deaths and partings. It endured, and made one ashamed, as if one watched a secret horror through a pierced wall, which is also theatre and part of its power to discomfort us. Here was the hypnotic spectacle of another's pain, solitarily suffered yet giving strength, for what McDiarmid dared and triumphed in, we also might. There was a full ten seconds here, but such an anatomy of anguish one watched as if a cadaver were flayed before our eyes by skilfully-wielded knives, showing us what lay horrifically beneath surfaces, an écorché of despairing life. The sob was precisely a sob. In its sculpting, its unearthly musicality, it contained what we know from *within* a sob to be. It was experience exemplified, a testamental moment, gathering to itself the history of every individual witnessing it, and therefore the greatest accomplishment of the actor's craft.

The development of a theory of beauty for the stage

Supplied	Denied
Poetry and metaphor	Accessible meaning
Speculation on behaviour	Routine moral assertion
Psychological unreliability	Recognizable human types or political stereotypes with value
Complex syntax	Naturalism or Realism
Long speeches	Familiarity, broken exchanges
The eruption of alternative discourses *within* the speech	Narrative in the speeches
Moments	Objectives
The gaol	The room
The spoiled landscape	The garden
The cemetery	The market
Pain at the insubstantiality of values	Affirmation of values
Melancholy	Love fulfilled
Non-therapeutic	Functional rewards
Non-enlightened	Socially improving
Constant digression	Plot
Accumulation of feelings	Development of argument
Complication	Critique
Irresolution	Solution
Disintegration	Restoration of self
Impossibility	Recognition

Towards a theory of production

What is the theoretical basis of The Wrestling School? In its inception, its posture was oppositional, inevitably since it had chosen to dedicate itself to the work of an author repudiated by the national companies, but more than this, oppositional since what aspires to be new desires the annihilation of the old, and the old had anaesthetized theatre, making it a 'vehicle' for 'truth' when the School already doubted 'truth' and saw the play as a vehicle for nothing but itself.

Its starting principles related to the complexity of its chosen texts, the explosion of which dictated the manner of production and its values. These texts were texts of ideas perhaps, but, more crucially, texts of emotions. The emotional range of these demanded a special discipline in actors, since the Barker play never denies articulation, is not repressive, implicatory or suggestive but describes, expostulates, seduces, language is the means by which the characters repel the misery of existence, and in the beauty of their speech, through both poetry and abuse, will themselves new life. Speech therefore, the mastery of rhythm, the passionate plasticity of language, was its first requirement in the actor. These actors, in understanding rhythm, understood also meaning, for the rhythm released meaning. The actors were in this liberated from the dead routines of the domestic and the urban, reported speech, documentary speech. Their voices were restored to them and this alone electrified an audience for whom theatre's poetry had long been denied in the pursuit of a political aesthetic.

But speech had been exemplary before. What therefore did The Wrestling School bring to the speech that made it resonate beyond the actor's individual powers? The production of the play had to match the ambition of the text, which was not self-aware. Few texts possessed so little self-awareness, of purpose, function, intention or end. The Wrestling School text is for nothing but its own witnessing. It is too full for comprehension on any but the most emotional levels of perception. Only a pitch of emotional complexity could overwhelm the resistances of an audience educated in the disciplines of meaning and the habits of entertainment. The culture is not neutral, but flogs its publics into obeisance to governing modes, political, aesthetic systems of seeing, hearing, demanding. What therefore, could be the sufficient context for such plays as these, which denied at the outset the rights of the existing order? The reinstatement of beauty within a world of pain, the repudiation of austerity, the creation of visual metaphors whose melancholy lay essentially in a decay, and the aggregation of a musical score whose ambition gradually rose to equal the ambition of the text itself, give The Wrestling School a context of such sympathy that the violent, disordered, broken narratives of the production are unified, contradiction exemplified as grace, and the whole experience immunized against the cramping verdicts of a utilitarian critical ideology. Is this a fantastical theatre? Emphatically not. For fantasy aspires to the eradication of all pain, a drunkenness for the world-weary. The play of The Wrestling School requires nothing of the impossible, but insists on the far reach of the possible, its speculations far outstripping tolerance, its imagination too unstable for enlightenment. It proclaims the world unstable, but in the apertures of pain discovers beauty. The routine assurances of humanism are not to be discovered here ('Life's good for all that . . .') and death has powers banished from most arts. Yet it compels. The compulsion of this spectacle is its own morality.

Barely concealed irritation
– a critical encounter

Critic. Can we agree that the first duty of art is to communicate?

Dramatist. Not at all. Art has no duties, and therefore no order of duties.

Critic. Very well, but it must communicate, surely?

Dramatist. It does so, whether it aspires to or not. Any event communicates itself, even if it is senseless, the senselessness communicates itself. In the first instance, art exists.

Critic. Like a bus, a ship, an elephant exists?

Dramatist. No, because these are neither self-conscious nor contradictory. Works of art shimmer with self-consciousness, they are tentative, speculative, they create *anxiety* in the beholder. But they do not *will* communication, it is not a prima facie characteristic of their existence. That they do communicate something – almost certainly distortion – is an effect of their subjectivity encountering the subjectivity of the beholder. What strikes me as absurd, repressive and actually contemptuous is the idea of communication as *morality*.

Critic. So the audience is not to be catered for?

Dramatist. It is permitted to witness the work of art.

Critic. You make it sound like a privilege.

Dramatist. Exactly so.

Critic. And if it does not feel privileged?

Dramatist. It stays away.

Critic. It seems to me you do not value the audience greatly.

Dramatist. The audience are allies to works of art, but works of art do not exist for them, they are not the condition of the inception of works of art, which can and do exist without them. The absence of an audience from a theatre may condition a performance, but the experience exists, witnessed or not.

Critic. Perhaps you hold the audience in contempt?

Dramatist. On the contrary, it is you who implies contempt by assuming the audience requires the simplifications, recognitions and disciplines that constitute 'communication skills' in art forms. The infantile desire to 'communicate' conceals arrogance and patronage. I am thinking of imperatives to *clarify*, to *elucidate*, to *enlighten*, the prejudice that audiences are recruitable, molten masses in search of order and form which can be bestowed upon them by their intellectual masters. It is always the so-called Realists who are most anxious to package experience in this way, when we know that reality defies it. The primary and dominant relationship is between the dramatist and the world. The actor comes to the text that is the product of this collision, this misunderstanding (for all art is misunderstanding). The actor does not 'clarify' this, he presents it, in all its deformity, its lack of objectivity. He does so brilliantly, mesmerically, intuitively.

Critic. And he might perform in an empty room for all you care?

Dramatist. That is precisely the situation in which much brilliant work occurs. But the audience always exists for the work. It is actively in search of it. When it discovers it, it also discovers that certain rules of witnessing it are infringed. The audience is therefore under an onus to learn new ways of receiving it. It is not for the acting company to play new work by the old rules. This is a source of anxiety, obviously, and tension, even hostility. How else can the essentially problematic nature of the encounter be sustained? If it is easy it is meaningless, it is merely entertainment, massage, sleep-walking.

Critic. I find this idea of the theatre as a place of pain and frustration repugnant. I want to leave a theatre in a state of satisfaction, delighted and grateful.

Dramatist. What is being satisfied? For what are you grateful? I could propose a different set of criteria, such as ecstasy, wonder, the sort of confusion that accompanies the early stages of a love affair, sensations that are not inert as the ones you describe. In any case, how an audience leaves a theatre is its own affair and not a factor in the production process, which is concerned with creating autonomous works of art, not commoditizing imagination for a market.

Critic. When I go to a theatre I seek pleasure and edification. What's wrong with that?

Dramatist. You would not need to be a psychologist to know the source of pleasure might be the spectacle of pain. As for edification, the concept of 'learning' from the stage cannot any longer be seen as a simple process of didacticism. Artistic creation is so unstable that a theatre seems to me the last place you would go in order to 'learn' something. On the other hand, you might well discover something, but that discovery would be a private matter, the outcome of subjectivity stimulated by the incongruous or the contradictory. It would not necessarily be a moment shared with any other. I do not subscribe to the notion of collectivity in theatre audiences, it is another aspect of control, manipulation, even a manifestation of a corrosive 'goodwill'.

Critic. This all seems to me to boil down to an elaborate justification of obscurity. What is the use of something that cannot be understood?

Dramatist. What you characterize as obscure is anything that does not belong among the given, the visible, the tangible, the existent, the authentic, the apparently true, the recognizable and the familiar. A theatre that has no truck with the 'obscure' is like a game of cards – the dealing of known emblems and numbers, entertaining but enervating, predictable even in its unpredictability (the shuffle changes the order). Speculative art, which is ipso facto obscure, expresses not so much the *unknown*, as the *unannounced*. This is creative anxiety. As for its use, utility has nothing to do with art. Art is strictly useless, which is its rebellion.

[137]

Critic. Who would want to see work of this nature?

Dramatist. In the last analysis, it is not a want, but a need. The theatre must apply itself to a need, and leave wants to the entertainment industry. Work of the kind I am describing often leaves its audience speechless – there is a failure of speech to accommodate what has been seen, which is the confirmation of success in isolating itself from existing critical categories.

Critic. And this speechlessness, this impossibility of enjoyment, or accommodation, whom does it help?

Dramatist. Helping strangers is not the function of art. The theatre is not a clinic, nor is drama a therapy for social malformation. Are there not enough life-improvers but you want them to own the theatre? The audience that is drawn by this work comes precisely to escape the doctrinaire impulse you want to inflict upon it.

On plethora

The work of art is not digestible
but
overwhelms
systems of consumption
evaluation
use
repair

The ordering of experience
is
posterior
not
anterior
to
the event

Therefore the artistic experience
must be new
in form

In the era of
access
bowdlerization
democratic simplification
only
plethora
refutes accessibility

Plethora
is
the art of excess
made necessary by the
so discreet provision of subject matter
relevance
conscience
and
tastefulness

Excess is the enemy of taste
not tastelessness

In excess
theatre proclaims its divorce
from
the myth of ordered life

Too many narratives
too many digressions
too many themes
being the condition
of
willing surrender

The play of plethora
being a poem
cannot be reduced
not being
a communiqué
cannot
be
abbreviated
acknowledged
or
approved

It
is not a despatch from a battle
delivered by an actor on a horse
('the writer says to advance!')

But
a flood
breaching the dike
of
common experience
and
inundating
the ordered pasture
of
communicable material
(society)

Goya's grin*

Goya's grin is the repudiation of the Enlightenment, a rebuke to reputation, a treachery. The idea of the responsible artist, the heroic critic and conscience of his age, is abolished in his collusive glance. On this preposterous image I based my libretto for Nigel Osborne's *Terrible Mouth*.

Goya has become in popular perception all things liberal and humane, moving through horror with an inspired pen, satirical of monarchs, priests and power, a suitable recruit to the progressive school of culture which sees all presentation of the cruel as a plea for peace from damaged sensibility.

Thus, the showing of all war becomes by extension, pacifist – the more the horror, the more certain the inducement to hate all violence. But the psychology of witnessing is more contradictory than this, and art's more powerful effects, in painting or theatre, come through ironic disjunctions, subterranean journeys through prejudice and instinct, ungovernable, immune to exhortation.

Goya, like the makers of all great artistic experience, is as untrustworthy as his self-portrait suggests, a man not more repelled than fascinated by disorder and sudden death.

If the greatest artistic experience lies in such ambiguity, the slip between will and desire, then good intentions have pitifully little influence here. It is the seduction of the artist by his own subconscious and the courage to yield to an imaginative extremity that distinguishes the great text – and the great performance – from the decent educators to whom we pay official homage, a false gratitude to moralists who struggle to keep our imaginations clean.

Moral instruction is the characteristic form of Reformation culture, and English art abounds in teachers, from More to Orwell, from Bunyan to the Royal Court. Methodism, the legitimizing ideology of Empire, social aesthetics and populist collusion require the work of art

* First published in *The Guardian*, 9th July 1992.

to 'function' critically or (the same thing) to function in the interests of harmony, utilitarian to the core.

In England, pain ceased to be fascinating with the death of Webster, and come the Enlightenment, theatre aspired to teach us manners, a pretention it has never forsaken. The urge to educate, elucidate, transform, so readily springing from the lips of dramatists, renders tragedy impossible, when tragedy is the art form of resistance in an age like this.

To write tragedy, to paint calamity, is to know the ambiguity that lies behind the witnessing of pain, the possibility of beauty in suffering – not as a political fetish – but within the privileged and illusory space of theatre, where theatre is emphatically not the world but a speculation upon it.

Tragedy is heresy in the populist state where politics is unanimous in its concern with the aggregation of satisfactions and where art, limping behind the unwieldy cornucopia of 'the good life', fears to arouse bad passions. Thus, the best bargain to be looked for in theatre is 'controversy', a sterile quarrel about the institutions of the state derived from the cult of critical realism.

'The author is criticizing …' says the satisfied customer. 'His message is …' relates the critic, a melancholy inheritance of 'objectives' derived from Brecht, Stanislavsky, and the English materialist school. But in contemporary society, everything is known, no one suffers in silence, access is all, and the trumpeting of grievances is the music of populism itself. To affirm our pleasures in collectivity we require a National Music Day.

Only in the hinge of conscience and collusion can be discovered the profane unease that is the real resource of tragedy, for tragedy is the assertion of self over collectivity, where pain and eros are licensed outside the trim gardens of sympathy or pornography. Is there greater erotic power than that which lies entwined in *Macbeth* or *King Lear*? And Goya's *Caprichos* with their young women, hags and roué customers, testify not to the moralizing satire of the Hogarthian school, but to the pain of an incurable wanting never diminished by age, the relentless pursuit of beauty as a refuge from despair.

Art does not educate, for to educate is to simplify. Art complicates the world, and the artist is the exemplification of the bad teacher, who in spite of himself, for all his mischief, cannot but tell a truth. What if Stendhal was a Bonapartist, Dostoevevsky a Slav Imperialist, or Celine a racist? Goya's grin reminds us not to trust the ostensible. The excavation of an artist's political or psychological character tells us nothing,

[142]

unless we persist in the infantile desire to be taught, and taught by saints.

Absolute illusion, the moment the artist or performer has full autonomy, abhors the 'dramatizing' of things (the verb itself a denial of drama) revealing that disloyalty to conscience that occurs when feelings are explored beyond the point of social legitimacy. At this point, art intoxicates its audience, troubling its convictions and placing dramatic experience at the centre of life, touching it at its most tender points and making it, not entertainment, but entertainment's opposite – necessity.

'I love what I hate. I have deceived myself.' Goya's apology.

Ignorance and instinct
in the Theatre of Catastrophe*

The Theatre of Catastrophe takes as its first principle the ignorance of the dramatist. This is not a statement of humility. On the contrary, it is assumed as a right and a privilege, the doorway to a reconstructed theatre.

How does this ignorance recognize itself? In the first place, it is an ignorance of social utility. The theatre has no use. Once this uselessness is recognized, the theatre is freed from its bondage to value. It no longer requires to be justified in the terms of the market. It is liberated from all commoditization. It is also freed from the burden of education and reform. It conceives itself in terms of *necessity* and not utility. It is no longer obliged to justify itself by its ends. It is for itself. It is neither profit nor therapy; neither entertainment nor enlightenment.

Second, this ignorance is recognized as a source of vitality. If the drama is to be more than the routine representation of contemporary fallacies, the thing called Critical Realism, it cannot know itself, nor can it be regulated. A regulated theatre is dead, whether that regulation arises from conscience or commerce. The essential creative element in theatre above all other art forms is its permanent *unreliability*, its incorrigible *instability*. This instability is exuded by the actor but it must originate in a text which is *unknowable*. The knowable text is thin, benign, complacent, propaganda or massage. It creates no problem for the actor, and worse, no problem for the audience. The actor does not suffer the ordeal of presenting the incongruities, the illogicalities, of the text, which is the source of a triumphant performance. The actor is primary in theatre because he alone has the power to make human the ostensibly inhuman elements of the Catastrophic play. This must be an ordeal for him. If the actor is not experiencing the ordeal of presenting the character, the experience of tragedy does not occur, for tragedy is plethora – it is the *unbearable* – literally, what *cannot be borne*, what cannot be carried and which spills, which falls to the ground and is seized

* Given as a paper at the University of Heidelberg ,18th June 1993.

[144]

up again, like a woman struggling with the too-many burdens of the refugee … this failure to transport the load is the ecstasy of Catastrophic tragedy.

Ignorance therefore is the first condition of a creative theatre. The dramatist renounces his educational presumption, his moral vocation. He confesses the poverty of his moral resources – a little disingenuously, for he suspects all those who declare themselves in possession of such things – and affirms that his sole right to the attention of an audience lies in his imaginative powers, the demonstration of which, through the voice and body of the actor, becomes a *need* and not a luxury, a *passion* and not a branch of the leisure industry, *instinct* and not the sterile debate of the education system. The dramatist and the actor refute the claims of all systems to possess their bodies and imagination. By this essential denial of incorporation they assert the historic function of drama as *chaos* and break its bonds with entertainment, the domesticization of art for the purposes of social control and edification.

I have said this crucial ignorance alone can make the theatre *necessity*. Why? The answer lies in the cultural superfluity of the modern era. Theatre is no longer capable of entertainment, despite its continual degeneration into the *realm* of entertainment. It is no longer possible to make it product, despite being part of mechanistic production processes, (e.g. National theatres …) and it is *perfectly inefficient*, the worst nightmare of accountancy. That is its profound redemption. In comparison with technological forms, information-systems, the capitalisation of education, the relentless flow of life-imitation and fantasy available on television and film, it asserts its problematic nature and resists incorporation by its very *form*. And beyond this … wherever theatre offers itself as entertainment it reveals itself as *degradation* even in the eyes and ears of unknowing audiences who desert the theatre and continue to desert it the more slavishly theatre attempts to win them by catering for its perceived taste. Another triumph of human nature over the market. Another triumph for the soul over the ethics of pleasure. Precisely because such a theatre is audience-led it is doomed to extinction. The demise of such a theatre should be welcomed as the peace of death gives welcome relief to an incurably suffering man. We assert the contrary practice. The theatre which is to be *necessity* repudiates the audience as the gratifying principle of production. It exists for itself, and paradoxically, by existing for itself it becomes a necessity for an audience for the reason that men and women ache for the representation of tragedy – which is pain – and this secret longing for the *incom-*

prehensible nature of pain – is beyond politics, beyond social order, and beyond conscience. It is *instinct*. Incomprehensible pain – the ignorant text – is loathed by society as society loathes instinct itself; society has an institutional investment in the eradication of pain and the elimination of tragedy from the sphere of art. Tragedy is inherently irrational, it affirms the *limits of social action* and therefore is fundamentally immune to the propaganda of the state and the revolution alike. It is no surprise then, that in an age of ideology and welfare the conventional wisdom has been that tragedy is impossible. No surprise either, that the dominant forms of popular theatre have been comic or musical, and no wonder still that governments and their allies in the leisure industry have tried to smear tragedy as 'pessimistic' and 'elitist ...' two terms we would be wise to adopt, cherish and advertize.

Let me summarize the argument so far. The sterility of the contemporary theatre, and its imminent extinction, follows from the theatre's sense of itself as an industry with a market, on the one hand, or a social service with a popular obligation, on the other. Let us call this the right and the left, if we must employ political formulations. Both of these positions require that the dramatist satisfy an audience in its perceived *demands* – entertainment or education. In attempting to satisfy these demands, the theatre slavishly performs functions more efficiently provided elsewhere and diminishes its particular powers, poetry, the spoken voice, the hypnotism of the actor. The Catastrophic Theatre on the other hand, does not address itself to demands at all. It does not invoke the audience as a justification for its existence. It *assumes* the audience, and paradoxically, by *assuming* it, it appears. Why does it appear? Because the tragic theatre speaks to needs which are not articulated in the wider culture, primarily the need for pain, and pain is the secret necessity on which tragedy builds its imaginative world.

The Theatre of Catastrophe therefore is ignorant of function, of *utility* and instinctive in its operations. How can such a theatre exist in a society obsessed with profit and enlightenment, with populism and access, where nothing is private and where the personal is perceived as something to do with bodily hygiene, where solitude is scarce and the secret exists only to be violated? It is not an easy task to invent the circumstances in which such a tragic vision might be permitted to exit. But certain forms suggest themselves.

Metaphorically, ignorance was associated with darkness, and by extension, enlightenment with light. Small wonder then, that Brecht ordained white light as the condition for his didactic theatre. Light on

[146]

the stage, and light in the audience. Thus we can be made to discipline ourselves. But the tragedy, disliked by Brecht and mischievously associated by him with despotism, prefers darkness, if only to separate the audience from itself, and oblige the *individual* to confront the pain on the stage in isolation. So this theatre will turn its back on the street, and the theatre walls will have both symbolic and practical significance. The walls will establish that the event about to be witnessed is secret, and what is more, *inaccessible*. Unlike street theatre, unlike the carnival, unlike the national theatre with its political objectives and its false unities, this theatre does not proclaim its universality at all. It is non-participatory in the social project, consequently its aesthetic principles must be *pessimistic* and *obscure*. How could it be optimistic without condoning the values of the system outside? How could it be accessible without transgressing its own rules? It will endure the hostility of the official theatre and earn the applause of the individual on whom theatre wholly depends – the actor, for he or she perform the secret life, which is their vocation. How often the actor is *employed* – what other word is there for his servile labour – on projects of pseudo-art ...? How rarely is he *licensed* to transgress?

I am describing here a process of *illegality*, for the Theatre of Catastrophe, like all illegal things, exists not on the surface, but in the interstices of culture. It does not advertize itself. It meets in unholy places. And whilst it does not humiliate its audience or offend it by intention, nor does it invite the audience to act critically either towards the production or the text, but rather it overwhelms the audience by the *plethora* of what it experiences. The sense of witnessing *too much*, of being *out of control* is essential to the Catastrophic play, which as in all other respects, rejects the socially-acceptable subject matter and the socially-acceptable duration of experience ... it has a vastness and disjointed character which defies all clarity. This quality of plethora invites new ways of seeing and witnessing since lineal narrative is regarded as reactionary and the experience is one of constant digression and a multitude of spectacles which are related not by theme but by tension, psychology or atmosphere. In my play of seven hours, *Rome*, the story of Abraham and Isaac is re-told in four different ways at different points, a French aristocrat in the middle of the revolution defends his culture in four different ways, and a Pope who, because of his passion for a woman's arse, cannot die even though he is fatally ill, persistently interrupts the action of the play to beg his mistress to commit suicide in order that he might find peace. None of these elements is logically connected.

[147]

Only when an audience renounces its trained, servile attitude to narrative and its critical-realist habits, both aspects of the entertainment/education complex of the culture industry, can it come fully to work of this kind. And what is its response? 'I was lost ...' resolves itself into 'I did not *know* what I was seeing, nor did I *enjoy* what I saw, but I want to experience it again ...' In this remark, the two principles of the Theatre of Catastrophe are unintentionally endorsed. At the same time, two rejections of populist aesthetics are articulated. *Not to know* admits a willing surrender of the critical faculty beloved of educational theatre ... *not to enjoy* announces a fracturing of the transaction values of the entertainment industry. On such statements of will, desire and bewilderment, the new theatre establishes its repertoire.

Why I am no playwright*

Samuel Clegg, Poet Laureate, High Tory iconoclast, protector of radicals, and failed dramatist, is perhaps the most entirely sympathetic character in *Victory*, but the reasons for his lamentable lack of success in the theatre might be examined in a broader context than the notorious Cromwellian ban on public performance.

Clegg's masterpiece, *Mayhem in Attica*, is a text that is doomed to expire unseen in the intoxicated air of a Restorian society already infatuated with entertainment, in this regard a sufficiently apt paradigm for the contemporary condition. What is Clegg's problem? Why does his text remain permanently on the desk of the Artistic Director of Drury Lane? His enemies might quote his rhyming couplets as damning evidence of a modest talent. His rebarbitive tone might be adduced as evidence why an audience would experience unease. And as for his politics, are they not a kettle of contradiction, turbid, baffling, prejudiced and inhumane? The inevitable conclusion will be that Samuel Clegg requires to learn the disciplines of the stage. The dramaturg will suggest politely that he attends a class. At some future date, it is possible a re-written version of *Mayhem in Attica* may reach the stage ...

Victory is not the most complex play I have written. With the passing of time, and the erosion of a whole range of political postures that appeared incontrovertible at the time of its creation, it appears if anything, increasingly lucid. If its first production was the result of good fortune, its second was the acknowledgement of its status as a text which is immune to a single political reading and permanently heretical in terms of its attitude to man. The problems surrounding its first production reflected the state of consciousness regarding theatre and its function at that time. Its subsequent celebrity reflects the changed nature of that consciousness. Both then and now *Victory* could not be viewed as a playwright's play.

It is theatre's own misfortune to have recurrent and illicit relations

* Given as a paper at the University of Cork, 28th October 1993.

[149]

with the entertainment industry. The most ardent practitioner of a Severe Theatre is never beyond the seduction of what is blithely called *success*. Like an insecure lover, the theatre aches to gratify. In pursuit of this gratification, it denies itself. Some relic of the exchange-relation imposes an imaginary obligation to satisfy, a satisfaction that can in many aspects be achieved by time-worn mechanical functions. How often do we hear from the director's lips that a certain action or a certain scene does not *work*? What constitutes this *working*, and to what end is it required to *work*? In this one utilitarian concept we hear the centuries-long echo of an art form which sacrificed its promiscuous and wayward liberties for the functional rewards of social discipline, and one in which, in ceasing to be a poet, the dramatist became a playwright, an artisan rather than a visionary, an element of a production process with defined obligations and subject to governing laws.

The image of the playwright – now fostered by the teaching of playwrighting as *craft* – is of one skilled in the production of narratives, able, like a tailor, to cut and join, link up seamless structures and provide the raw material for the actor to demonstrate powers of speech and action. In this function he or she not only creates the text, but manipulates it in the service of the production. The suffix 'wright' in the word playwright, evoking workshops and muscularity, implicitly demands hard-headedness, practicality, the non-effeminate, all the catalogue of virtues belonging to honest labourers bent on *making* and unlikely to indulge in self-expression to any degree that would inhibit the process of manufacture. What does this functional character of the dramatist imply? First, in common with wheelwrights, shipwrights and millwrights, it implies the existence of a *market*, and theatre's ambiguous relations with the market have traditionally shaped its forms. Samuel Clegg's *Mayhem in Attica* is perhaps not so badly written as it is unmediated by its author's eye on market forces. A 'playwright' – which Clegg manifestly is not – has a product to sell. The very writing of his text would seem to presuppose an audience, and this audience has habits of perception, reflexes, expectations, which must be accommodated. Success is dependent on the satisfaction of these implicit demands. To return to a real play, *Victory* lacks the playwright's technique from the outset. The opening scene, far from setting out to win an audience with the traditional bait of theatre practice, appears to exert itself to create offence. Three factors combine to produce anxiety and distrust in an audience whose innocence is always – in a patronizing way – taken for granted. The subject matter is obscure. The discourse is in a form of English which is unfamiliar, and this unfamiliarity is startlingly ruptured by a torrent of only too familiar vituperation. This is bad playwrighting, though it is arguably good theatre, and if it is good theatre it is good for the reason that it abnegates the concept of satisfaction as a governing morality in dramatic art.

If *Victory* flouts the cherished conventions of narrative and taste, it is also an example of bad playwrighting in another regard, for if one of the *characteristics* of the dramatist is the crafting of the play for the market, a second is the relation of the text to morality, and the failure of *Victory* to endorse any political posture despite its intensely political milieu, contributed to its rejection by the main producing managements of the English theatre even where these establishments were not *prima facie* commercial – and in the case of the Royal Court, where a much-trumpeted 'right to fail' was inscribed in its aesthetic manifesto. The 'right to fail' did not incorporate a right to be without moral earnestness, however. *Success* in such a regime could not be popularity, but it might consist of the skill with which a moral posture was articulated. The *Playwright* is above all, a man or woman in the fullest accord with the moral ether which society breathes. Beside the skills in dialogue, the ear for the common speech of his fellows, the ability to stage an event, to run a narrative, the playwright *thinks in his time*, while the poet is essentially discordant.

There is one further sense in which the despised Sam Clegg might have discovered some compensations for his failure to see *Mayhem in Attica* staged. It may have been, in the convention of its time, *unstageable*, a peculiar notion which the playwright understands and the poet does not. The playwright's antennae are acutely angled to the audience at all times … he senses its alienation, he fears its boredom, he is for ever waiting to *amend*, to exploit or to cut a scene; for the playwright and his ally the director, the audience *lead* the production, and via the barometer of its satisfactions, simultaneously censor it. For the poet, his or her own experience is the pretext for the entire staging of the play, and as a consequence of this, the production cannot but be innovative, for the rules of the existing dramatic structures are infringed. Perhaps in any case, the audience is not bored, merely seething against itself. Perhaps its silence is not anger, but pain. Perhaps, whereas it came for pleasure, it has been granted the gift of melancholy instead, and finds this bewildering but not unwelcome. Because the audience dominates the playwright, he is unlikely to be the instrument by which theatre undergoes profound changes of function. The poet on the other hand, may lead the audience, albeit unwillingly, into new relations with the stage quite simply because he does not care about them, but regards them as privileged witnesses to a rare event.

Mayhem in Attica may have been a lost masterpiece. If *Victory* is a masterpiece, its survival has been the consequence of a coalition of fortuitous events that permitted both its first production and the play's revival nearly a decade later. Some of these events have their origins in the theatre itself: the breakdown of a company's planning schedule that required a play at a moment's notice; the inception of an acting company able to draw on the minimum resources of the state; some of the events were public, political, international – the mystery of relevances, when for example, the decay and collapse of state socialism in Eastern Europe imitated the climate of the text, freshened it, gave it the necessary pretext for revival. Because it originated with a dramatist who never addressed himself to *craft*, its problems as a play might have foredoomed it to permanent obscurity. How often have I been told that I had no understanding of structure; how often that I was spoiled by a taste for excess? The terms are meaningless to an artist who might as well be told that Picasso was for a long time dangerously obsessed with the colour blue. It is the habit of the playwright to interrogate himself for signs of excess, for lack of organizational ability and every flaw that might cost him that precious commodity that must be wrung from audiences – sympathy. But who would not happily exchange sympathy for compulsion? People have quit productions of *Victory* at every performance. Others have not. And others still have come again on subsequent nights. For these, *success* could not be measured in terms of pleasure, satisfaction or reward. For these, the old compact between theatre and audience – the delivery of gratification – no longer applied. Only by infringing the rules of playwrighting was the theatre able to shed its utilitarian functions and become – however briefly – unredeemed pain, a spectacle of suffering without moral rectitude, experience without order.

Murders and conversations: the classic text and a contemporary writer*

The highest pleasures of delinquency come from an affront to an authority that cannot be moved. To deface a monument, to smear a public property, is an act of reverence more profound, because of the investment of will, than any common genuflection of the uncritical believer. It is the continuity and immobility of things that supplies the authentic shock behind all acts of desecration.

Taking this to be a self-evident truth, my relations with a small number of classic texts have not been coloured by the natural resistance felt by living authors to the oppressive presence of masterworks now regarded as beyond criticism. Tolstoy's ranting against a Shakespeare he resented as a rival is a sufficient indication that any number of proofs cannot inflict lasting damage on cultural artefacts which are, by definition, not susceptible to argument. My approach has been stimulated by the individual text and the absences and silences within it, perceptions or quarrels that would be unlikely to arise in the minds of those who were not themselves makers of texts. Sometimes these resonant spaces, when investigated, have led me to an interrogation of the function of the text – and the cultural status of the author – in contemporary society, an elision which is perhaps inevitable in confronting authors who are now more significant than the sum total of their works. I am here thinking not so much of Shakespeare, now a negligible influence on the tone of contemporary writing in Britain – itself a tragedy for the theatre of our time – as Chekhov, whose uncontested authority in British theatrical and cultural circles has made of him a more luminous icon in this part of Europe even than in his country of origin.

What compels an author – at various moments in his progress – to engage in this literary necrophilia is in the broader sense, a matter of personal psychology. I have talked of the lacunae and silences apparent to me in the works of certain classic authors. Other writers would discover different ones, but in examining my own motives for returning

* Given as a paper at the University of Portsmouth, 7th December 1994.

rather frequently to what – depending on your point of view – is either the charnel house or the pantheon of European drama, I can discern at once that I am not compelled by the preposterous chimera of making old work 'relevant'. I have shunned relevance with every text I have written, which may explain the continuing relevance of them to cultural experience far beyond my own. If art is relevant to anything, it is so by accident, and its task is to survive its own relevance and lodge at some deeper stratum of consciousness, immune to time if not to idiom. The relevant is always transparent, instantaneous, facile, newsworthy – and, because art is essentially a mystery, to inject it with the stimulant of the modern is only to make it dance in a frantic and drug-addicted way. My motives have been both more and less reverential than the obsession with 'up-dating …'

The four occasions for what were, at the outset, forms of conversations with dead authors, were different in each case. In the first, an invitation to modernize Middleton's Jacobean classic *Women Beware Women* turned into a desire to redistribute the moral authority within the text, excavate the minor characters, and abolish a transparently inauthentic ending. I retained the whole power of Middleton's language and plot, but added a new act, thereby serializing it. In effect two plays were placed in juxtaposition, both morally speculative, both poetic in discourse. My encounter with Middleton was amicable, and uncoloured by any emblematic status within English culture, for the Jacobeans have never enjoyed the secure approval of the modern mind. My interrogation of Shakespeare's *King Lear* was not prompted by a spasm of feminist sensibility. What made me question the absence of Lear's wife from Shakespeare's tragedy was a writer's feeling for the architecture of a text, and we have slowly re-learned that architecture is about emptiness as well as substance, void as well as materiality. *King Lear* is about family, and family, whatever its origins as an economic contract or its prophylactic qualities as a counter to social decline, is also an emotional zoo of peculiar and agonized calls, suffocated appetite, barred cages, will without action, contrived blindness and organized repression. That Shakespeare was describing a primitive aristocracy does not detract from the enduring characteristics of marriage and paternity. I was compelled by an unhealthy curiosity to examine the character of Lear – perhaps the greatest tragic figure of the modern world – in the light of a repression, the murder of a mother in which an entire family participated. This speculation – in effect, a moral transgression erupting inside a known and to some extent, now *placid*, story, governs my description of the early life of Lear in the play *Seven Lears*.

My third engagement with a classic text is with Chekhov's *Uncle Vanya*, and most recently, I converted Gotthold Lessing's comedy *Minna von Barnhelm* into a tragedy. Both were at the outset conversations, but the more complex this dialogue was, the more heated it became, and just as an act of love contains the potential for an act of violence, so these meetings became collisions of a profoundly moral nature. And it is the mark of the enduring power of dead artists and the cultural investments made in them – for political and ideological reasons – that a living dramatist should be driven to acts of murder. For we are not solely engaged with a dead man or woman, whose personality is beyond our reach, but with the sordid utility value that is extracted from their labour. This extends beyond the field of drama itself, at least as far as my own work is concerned, and in the opera *Terrible Mouth* (composed by Nigel Osborne, performed at the ENO Almeida season of 1992) it was the socio-political crust inflicted on the painter Goya that prompted an angry meditation on a mysterious figure conventionally described as a paragon of radical, progressive, humanist inclinations profoundly horrified by everything he chose to paint, but who, it was felt by me, could not have been less than profoundly implicated in his own violence.

The classic text, whilst permanent, is never stable. Chekhov and Shakespeare may stand solid as ancient oaks, but as oaks change colour with the seasons, so texts alter their complexions with the passage of regimes. The life of a text is akin to the melancholy movements of a concrete edifice of Lenin, one day totem, the next flower-bedecked object of mild mockery in a fashionable restaurant, and soon to become the pretext for a revisited savagery. More sinister than the current obsession with 'relevance', the annexation of texts for political and social educational projects is well documented. Soviet versions of Chekhov emphasized – or invented – positive Marxian meanings from these inert texts, and Shakespeare has always been a source for transfusions of patriotic inspiration when a national crisis necessitated it. It seems possible to argue that it is this pliability of the text that, in the end, lends it its classic status, for all forms of society, and all modes of opposition, require the endorsement of smothered genius. Are we immune? Obviously not. Shakespeare will always be our contemporary for this reason: his texts are perpetually plundered by the existing dispensation whatever its current preoccupations. Thus the conversations

I describe with regard to Shakespeare, Chekhov or Lessing, are partly inspired by authorship, partly by the use to which these authors have been put by contemporary ideologues, and partly by my own resistance to the forces and inertias that govern the contemporary theatre.

All these elements contribute to the lethal conversation which informs my own *(Uncle) Vanya*. Chekhov's anti-tragic theatre has at its core a profound horror of melodrama, but a horror of melodrama might well disguise an unease with drama itself, which describes action and alteration, as Chekhov's theatre repudiates these things. The character Vanya – a Lear without the courage of his own imagination – pathetically fails to use a pistol effectively on the man he deems his worst enemy, thereby trapping himself in further descending loops of self-contempt. In making the bullets strike their target, my own version of the play launches the stagnated personality of Vanya on a course of decision – decision being the key to tragedy and a concept entirely absent from the Chekhovian world, for the word 'decision' means literally 'to cut', and cutting ends one life and compels the individual to reach for another.

There are probably rather few murders that do not have their origins in a conversation, and a conversation between strangers always contains the seeds of violence. In this instance, my attraction towards Chekhov for his greatly-imagined character turned into a resentment against the moral vacuity both within the text and in regard to its effect on the audience, and subsequently the mode of thinking surrounding much theatrical presentation in our own time. I have stated above that there seems no authentic energy to be released from the cult of modernization of classic texts, but by opening up the fissures of morality in the texts, the classic author and his modern equivalent might both be more brilliantly illuminated. The text is a site of struggle, neither sacred nor sterile, for over its surface run cracks and chasms, poorly-disguised faults and deep holes overlaid with thin crusts, swamps as well as granites. The author is never the strong man or woman he appears, never really the omnipotent conjuror, but rather an individual frequently afraid of the scale of his invention, timid for his reputation, and not immune from the terrible knowledge that imagination is without morality, an animal released and then collared again. Perhaps the spectacle of a mind as fine as Shakespeare's, or more pertinently, Chekhov's, shocked at the mayhem his dream might unleash, is more beautiful than the drama itself, and infinitely more dramatic, for Chekhov lent Vanya the pistol only to withdraw it again, and it is savage to show a man freedom only to slam the door in his face when he attempts to cross its threshold.

It is to this crisis of the imagination, concealed within structures that lend an artificial elegance, and encrusted with the approbation and religiosity of both state and academe, that my own conversation is addressed. When Shakespeare made Lear rage, did he not love him more than when, humiliated and broken by events, he brings him to the brink of an apology? Was Chekhov not charmed by Vanya's bitterness, and glimpsing his sexual power, locked it up again, like a shameful deformity? And how much broken will attaches not only to the characters of these plays, but to their creators? There is no answer to this question, but I raise it to suggest the intimacy that conditions the first conversations between a living and a dead artist, conversations which, as they unfold, might reveal not only the desire felt by one for another, but also the potential lethality of it, for there's no passion where the spectre of murder does not haunt the room.

By inflicting altogether different moral perspectives on texts such as *(Uncle) Vanya* or *King Lear*, does a modern author change the character of the original? Can an intervention by one artist in the territory of another be anything but a raid, an assault, a seizure of aspects of one cultural moment by the temper of another? How representative am I, in any case, of my own cultural moment? How much was Chekov? It's a tedious convention to believe we are all nothing but moving fingers for the social structures of our time, and a convention an artist – if he is to keep faith with his vocation – must resist. Vanya, in other words, Marxist testimony notwithstanding, did not have to be Vanya, for it is the moment of autonomy that makes the stage character resonate in the mind, and the sole claim of dramatic invention on the unwilling curiosity of an audience. We are free to invent, even if invention requires at times to be stimulated by obstinacy, irrational will or a heroic repudiation of our own fear and piety. The depth of social and political investment in classic texts, ironically enhanced by apparently daring 'modernizations', can only be properly shifted by an equivalent bravery made by a new interrogation. We then might glimpse the original text for the frail and naked exposition of feeling, tender and afraid, that it once was. In the mirror of a new Lear, an old Lear might be seen as an artist at bay, and in the new *(Uncle) Vanya*, the contempt of life that clings to the old might be exposed, like vestiges of ancient cultures, through the heavy clays of critical investment and political expediency.

What's new ...?*

'What's new ...?'

A muttered idleness between two individuals who long ago forsook all intimacy. A question which is not a question. A reflex. An interrogation without passion. A lethargy. The shoulder-shrugging attitude of populist culture limping from novelty to novelty. The hi or ciao of redundant etiquette.

And how to reply to what is not an authentic question? Nothing. Nothing is new. The new itself aches with senility, a faltering cadaver of frustrated hope and insipid delights, a roué staggering in the pleasure grounds of peace and plenty muttering its desperation for the spectacle that might delay its death. Time to tip the new into the grave it has always aspired to, which given its fragility, will require no effort. The word is dirty on the lips and disgusting to the ear, for these organs of sense know long before the mind the decay of a concept by its staleness, its bad odour.

Those uncontaminated by the sickness of the new might seek the thing the new knows nothing of, though it is itself not new, namely the *secret*, for in the age of transparency and total surveillance, the secret becomes simultaneously a privilege and a triumph, though not a right, for rights are no more than the orchestrated racket of dying democracies. The secret is necessarily criminal, the unjustifiable demand for *solitude*, consequently an illegality of mind. When the confession box is made of glass, it is time to love the dark. When the camera intrudes into the entrails, it is time to speak of death as a friend.

The secret is hated by the mob and hated by the state, allies in the perpetual war against difference. The secret shuns the light but is nevertheless violable, and must be violated, but no sooner is it violated than it takes up residence elsewhere, it is permanently fugitive, it makes elusiveness its special character, repudiating debate with its false claims to dialectic truths, and parodying the interrogation as a sterile collision

* Published in *Quoi de Neuf?*, University of Poitiers, 14th November 1994.

[158]

of diseased egos. Perhaps it cannot speak; certainly it lacks the *skills of communication* that distinguish and humiliate the media agent, the radical, the celebrity morbid with self-exposure. If the secret has a language it is a language that *excludes* and is consequently *uncommercial*, a language that remains obscure even to its acolytes, for at the moment they think they possess its character its character changes, for how could they continue to adore what they have found the key to? The secret above all things has to be adored, and this adoration takes the form of an anxiety to possess, akin to the sexual passion whose object, even while seduced, cannot be held, for the pain of desire lies beyond seduction, in the realm of *sustained obsession*.

Finally, the secret enrages. It enrages by its evasiveness, its refusal of access in an age of absolute visibility. Only to the few who hunger for it does it lend the power of desire. In other words, the secret divides, it abhors false unity, seeing unity as organized deception, a regime of slogans common to the anarchist, fascist, humanist and democrat alike. The secret is immaculate, and in absolute contradistinction to the *new* it has no desire to replace the existent with itself, the poverty of the existent being, after all, the condition of its own beauty …

Dog on stage

The public resents great art for its greatness as swiftly as it indulges poor art for its poverty.

This resentment against great art is the product of a dread, the sort of dread induced by proximity to a desired object, for it is a paradox that what we urgently desire, we also dread.

This simultaneous dread of great art and indulgence of the poor serves to shield the tenderness of compromise, the frailty of faith, the brittleness of conviction, from exposure to contradiction. Wherever an authentic work of art makes its first appearance, there is dread even where there appears only exhilaration.

In every journey to the theatre (we do not talk of *visiting* the theatre) there lingers the never-extinguished prospect of personal destruction, which is the nature of all supremely erotic encounters also. No one cares to express this, for who dares admit that she aspires to her own catastrophe? It is the erotic secret of tragedy.

Thus at those moments of immaculate exposure to seduction/destruction – instances of imminent nakedness – the audience seeks with desperation the means of its escape, the pretext by which it might evade the power of staged experience – the failure of a performance, a glaring weakness of the text, a technical breakdown, or the appearance on the stage of a stray animal which with its unerring instinct for the triggering of bathos, will deliver this audience from the brink of a greater chaos that that which its appearance might induce …

The glass confessional: the theatre in hyper-democratic society*

One of the many deceits that lie at the heart of theatre practice, and one to which it is specially susceptible, given its artistic form, is authorial invisibility. Whilst we who make texts expect to claim the credit for the achievement of a dramatic presentation, and equally expect to suffer the often violent repudiation of ourselves that attends on public scrutiny of this production, we are peculiarly absent at the moment of performance in a way which is untypical of other art forms. When we read a poem, the poet's identity is immediate, so intimate that we feel we are a collaborator in a struggle of articulation. When we read a novel, the nature of the narrative is such that we are constantly aware of the controlling and revealing hand of its creator. The painting is indelibly identified with an individual whose style – particularly in contemporary painting – is its whole raison d'Ítre. In theatre for the most part, the authorial identity is concealed by the mediation of actors, whose very function is to divert the attention of the audience away from its own manipulation, usually by one of the many practices and techniques that go under the name of Realism. In its more extreme varieties, this fiction of authorial absence leads to a spurious sense of objectivity that clings to the entire experience, such that the play degenerates into a debate, effectively de-fictionalizing itself and positioning the audience as consumers of enlightened truth dispensed by committees of researchers, workshop teams and devisers whose function is to manufacture seamless and non-eccentric narratives.

The more theatre took upon itself the critical function of exposing and describing everyday life, the more it had thrust upon it the intolerable onus of perpetual revelation of social scandal and political shortcoming. At its apotheosis of social responsibility, the dramatist came nearest to total obscurity, degenerating into a benign organizer of material, a self-selecting maker of testament, not to his or her own madness, but to the degeneration of social order. At the slightest whiff of perse-

* Given as a paper at the University of Birmingham, 13th March 1995.

[161]

cution, this individual could respond in the time-honoured way by arguing that he was merely holding up a mirror to society, as if in any meaningful sense, mirrors told the truth at all. The contemporary theatre is dominated by a principle of lucidity, both in terms of its product in techniques – a sort of pre-Freudian clarity derived from Brecht and Stanislavsky – and in terms of its material, which is unrelentingly journalistic in its appetite for exposure, revelation and inevitably, with the degeneration of journalism itself – scandal.

We required Michel Foucault to elaborate what most Europeans have always suspected about dark places and speaking, that confession comes easiest in the dark, and that it is vastly more sexually stimulating to tell than to keep silent. The oscillating character of self-revelation, the urge to confess – powerful as the urge to transgress, but complicated by the vertigo of confession itself into exaggeration and unmitigated lying – makes the confession box of the Roman Catholic church, for all its antiquity, an apposite paradigm for an alternative theatre practice to the one described above. If in the confession box the subject is obliged, privileged, and indeed compelled to be indiscreet to the point at which a challenging and erotic relation is sustained with a listening ear, the theatre, a place equally dark and with a different listening ear, multiple yet simultaneously individual, might also become a place of mutual seduction in which the category truth is only ostensibly the pretext for the encounter.

However, nothing does, or ever has, stood still in the Roman Church, and the discarding of the Latin mass, a sufficient metaphor for the command of populist society, that everything shall be understood by everyone and that nothing – least of all a language – shall be the property of a few, provides another image of theatre practice, where language also has become unspecific to itself, street language, no longer specially construed for its milieu. But the Roman Church's passion for modernity has recently spawned an innovation more startling than this, a phenomenon far-reaching in its implications not only for religious practice but for the parameters of social and private space, and one therefore, highly relevant to any discussion of theatre. This is the glass confessional.

Let us rehearse the historic function of confession, which for all its parallels with psycho-analysis, is one of the most ancient rituals of Christianity. It is first and foremost a moment of profound self-examination, in which the supplicant, requiring to relieve him or herself of a perceived sin, employs the mediation of a priest to intercede with God in order to be forgiven, discharged of guilt and returned to society in a fit condition to share in the blessings of mankind. That authentic confession is an ordeal should be self-evident. That the experience is liable to degeneration is equally obvious, and degeneration is at least as interesting as authenticity from the artistic or cultural point of view. But to remain within the realm of intentions for the time being, certain circumstances were deemed essential for the act of confession, conditions under which truths difficult to communicate might be expressed, for expression – *telling* – is the purpose, *knowing* merely the preparation for telling. The first of these was seclusion. Just as the psychiatrist's couch is no innocuous space, but a contrived environment of hierarchy and order – one needs only to see Freud's Vienna consulting room to recognize the infinite attention paid to details of status, imagery, furnishing, and so on – so the classic confessional is situated in a side aisle, curtained, and so immune to interference by third parties that a red light is displayed to deter accidental intrusion. The tenderness entailed in articulating a sin – the authentic agony experienced by a man or woman burdened with shame – is catered for by a structure of intimacy and privacy in which even the features of the priest are concealed by a grille. Taken as a whole, the confession box might be thought of as one of the highest imaginative manifestations of a disciplined but contemplative society, tender yet cruel, sensitive yet authoritarian, a brilliantly evolved machine of freedom and order. The regulatory regime of confession is a keystone to the structure of theocratic power. Yet at the moment of confession it is simultaneously the epitome of privacy in self-exposure. Privacy, is however, the cardinal sin of the populist moment in democratic evolution. Hence, the visitor to the church of Saint Sulpice in Paris ought not to be surprised to find the new confessional is made of glass.

What can be deduced in terms of social and political development from this absolute reversal of the terms of one of the most ancient conventions of European culture? For the application of the principle of transparency to this formerly sacred occasion is precisely *absolute* reversal; the priest is visible to the penitent; the penitent is visible to the priest; both are visible to the public. Only one aspect of the private nature of confession is preserved – it remains inaudible. But for how much longer? The dumb show of a person's pain, already attracting a curious audience, can only benefit from the addition of the dialogue. It is tempting to think this innovation was the church's attempt to lay low the centuries-old comic image of the lascivious priest exciting himself in the darkness while a young woman confesses her thoughts, but there is something more compelling entailed in the regime of transparency, which is the simultaneous hounding of the secret and the conversion of all human activity to the realm of entertainment.

It has long been a tenet of democratic societies – and an obsession in revolutionary ones – that those who required privacy had something to conceal, that secrets are privileges and therefore a contempt of the people, and that openness, seemingly an unimpeachable virtue, justifies permanent scrutiny, a policing of private life not by the church but by the investigative journalist. It was the first revolutionary democracy of 1789 that incorporated the journalist into an agent of the state, and the French Revolution also that invented the show trial. In the case of Marie Antoinette, the show trial was converted into pure entertainment by the hysteria of the press and its flood of faked revelations about the secret life of the monarchy, its debauched sexual appetites, and so on … the now familiar necessity to smear as well as convict. By the time of Stalin's purges, a bizarre twist was lent to the show trial by the semi-religious ritual of the public confession, but the heart of the entertainment remained the exposure of the secret. It is perhaps not surprising that an institution so subtly attuned to the political currents of its time, and supremely preoccupied with surveillance as the Roman Catholic Church, should have embraced the glass confessional with the onset of social transparency, and only surprising that it took so long. It is after all, supreme entertainment; just as in the quiz game the contestant feels constrained to make a clown of herself, so in the glass confessional the penitent cannot resist the temptation to act up, since she now attracts an audience outside the glass to whom an obligation is necessarily owed. The tendency to exaggeration always existed in the confessional, but now the priest also must give a *performance*, and we – fascinated observers – become that most beloved unit of entertainment in hyper-democratic culture – *participants*.

All of this has much to do with the theatre, in so far as the theatre, like the church, resonates to the prevailing ideology. If, as I have predicated, we live in a cultural moment of Absolute Access, the complete abolition of private space – and I include the sexual body, now the subject of universalization, another commodity for seizure and revelation, rape and the photojournalist – then the theatre, always susceptible to its innate oppositional instincts, might rediscover one of its prime resources, long since smothered as an embarrassment during the years of enlightenment: its power to corrupt.

[164]

As long as theatre perceived itself – in the wake of Brecht, Shaw, and the Royal Court's Theatre of Conscience – as the supreme edifier, its unhealthy utilitarianism could never be shed. It was required to justify itself by results, the casting of light into dark corners, the clarification of social problems, the 'raising of consciousness', all acts of illumination, revelation and – the word has to be used – strenuous efforts towards the dissemination of 'truth'. But revelation has expired when everything is revealed. In a social climate obsessive with transparency, the theatre's old compact with darkness might lend it a power it has prematurely abandoned. Is it not, in any case, structured for secrecy? Brecht notwithstanding, is it not compulsively dark? Is it not, in its relation with the world, private space, walled, enclosed, privileged by the small numbers it can serve, if not by its price? And finally, is it not peopled by actors, the least trustworthy of human beings by common accord of nearly every culture, individuals possessed of a sinister craft so seductive (hence, illogical and un-transparent) that in Christian culture at least, they were denied burial in hallowed ground? This inherent and implicit secrecy of form must have recommended itself to de Sade, who we know, in the strictly inaccessible confines of his estate, organized a theatre of his own. De Sade's secrets were of course, intolerable to absolutism and revolution alike. His texts now possess precisely the character of *exposed* secrets, disturbing, unstable and probably un-annexable.

Let me pose the oscillation of the secret – its painful fascination – in a recollection of common childhood experience. We recall how as children we felt a peculiar resentment against a certain other child who appeared to be in possession of knowledge we were not party to; he or she *would not tell*. To make this child *tell*, to reveal its privileges, all sorts of tortures were devised. By contrast to this fury of persecution, to be in *possession* of a secret was a kind of ecstasy, which if shared with another (probably the most ecstatic moment of all) was done circumspectly, with the absolute inhibition on communicating it any further … yet more ferocious punishment 'if you tell …'. Telling or not telling, revelation or silence, the social and the private in a vertigo of seduction and punishment. This is potentially the ground for an aesthetic of theatre in an age of ostensible truths, total exposure and withering enlightenment. And theatre is probably better equipped for this secretive, evasive, anti-utilitarian aesthetic than any other form. Its store of techniques include the chorus, the aside, the soliloquy, rhetoric, a poetic idiom, symbolism, any number of forms of realism, an unparalleled range of mimetic devices which enable it to pose modes of existence, options for existence, which the great industrialized modes of entertainment can neither appropriate nor match. In its long and arguably fruitless obsession with the social-realist mode, theatre abandoned almost every technique that distinguished it from television or film – even if to a considerable extent it could pride itself on the dubious distinction of having pioneered many televisual practices in the first place.

What might be the character of a Theatre of Secrets? Having outlined the social context that seems to me propitious for its announcement, it is possibly premature to attempt an articulation of its form, but certain distinct possibilities suggest themselves. One of these must be its repudiation of fact, a resolute disinclination, a sense of the unhealthiness not of the world but of the so-called facts of the world, for the facts of the world are the property of information industries, critical journals, history seminars, news programmes and the like. A theatre which sets out to reveal the facts of the world is a disarmed theatre, already marginalized by technologies beyond its power to imitate. On the other hand, a theatre which invents the world (And the objections of the realist audience that 'this couldn't happen to me', 'this never happened to me', 'This won't happen to me', are reservations of no intrinsic value) provides a speculative forum of human behaviour which must take its incomprehensibility for granted – a sign of struggle, anxiety, even dismay, and certainly embarrassment, the particular form of embarrassment that attends on the new whenever it appears in an authentic form. Any work of art that de-stabilises the cherished moral convictions of an audience will produce embarrassment, if only because – like a blush – a secret thought collides with public decorum. This embarrassment may of course – again like a blush – be a manifestation of a pleasure that can't be announced. It is on this fine point of corruption that a Theatre of Secrets will require to stand – infinitely poised – for the theatre has rarely been more vulnerable, and rarely required to draw on so many of its resources to survive.

That this theatre will also be a theatre of text is fully contingent on some of the premises already described. If it is to articulate the secret it must do so in a language of secrets, a language which is not primarily concerned with the patina of social discourse – the conventional speech of transaction, communication, clarity, ostensible meaning – but a form which brings to the surface – erupts from beneath the surface – the normally *unspoken*, the counter-discourse, the private, that which is not, in a Stanislavskyan sense, an *intention* at all, but a diversion. This language – almost certainly poetic in form, if only as a consequence of being *invented* – will be in contradistinction to the theatre language of realism, saturated with its author's personality, a language in which the anonymity of the author – a facet of modern theatre I referred to at the opening of this paper – will be impossible to sustain, abolished by that eccentricity of tone that distinguishes all poetry. An audience will sense the total lack of objectivity, the startling absence of judgement, implicit in what it witnesses and hears. Far from feeling itself the subject of an episode of enlightenment, safe in the hands of a self-proclaimed moralist (an author) it will sense the terrible insecurity of being invited by a highly suspicious individual known as an actor, to become party to a secret, to share a transgression, in a darkened room. The more blinding the transparency of a cultural ethic, the more subtly authoritarian its surveillance/entertainment axis, the harder this invitation will be to refuse.

Disputing Vanya*

Comedy's perpetual failure lies in its inducement to love, turning the scorned character into a treasured partner of our frailty. Thus it is that aborted life exemplified on stage might be seductive in itself, not a needle stuck in the conscience ('I could be other than this ... !') but welcome assurance we also need never shift ('It's too much for *all* of us ...'). Beyond this, the odour of the Chekhovian room, stale with frustrated decision and annihilated will, becomes peculiarly sweetened by the assigning of spiritual wealth to impotence, a perverse approval of moral suicide concealed behind gentle manners, civil concession, the tears of things ...

The humanist gesture is more accompanied in Chekhov's *Uncle Vanya* than in any text made not only by him but by his numerous heirs and imitators. And Vanya is, in the pathos of his petulance, supremely the humanist individual, a martyr to civility and suffocated instinct, self-effacement and the responsibilities of love. His mutinies, inept, humiliating, serve only to shorten the rope from which he dangles, and his rages only consume a stunted self-esteem. In social moments vastly different from that which we now live, Vanya might have trod the line of the clown, contemptible, an admonition against wrong life, but the most manipulative director working in a climate of unbridled idealism or political exigency would still discover in this text such perfect pity that Vanya's melancholy martyrdom – this is no tragedy, after all – would shimmer through the densest fog of ideological interpretation. Furthermore, this is a great actor's role – one of the half-dozen in the modern canon – and we know the endorsement brought to character by the application of talent and distinction. Moral failure in the hands of a master becomes a terrible charm.

Uncle Vanya has been so thoroughly aired on the English stage in recent years, as well as being filmed twice in the English-speaking world in the same period, that its appeal can only be located in its comforting

* First published in *The Guardian* under the title 'Subverting Vanya', 17th April 1996.

denigration of heroism, its by-passing of moral will and the aestheti-
cization of stasis which accords with a social climate itself embarrassed
by personal autonomy, willing itself into conformity and charmed by
the spectacle of the unshakeable power of the domestic. It is perhaps
the function of the classic work to act precisely as this source of collective reassurance, moving from obscurity to prominence and back again
as the state of society bestows significances never predicted or intended
in the moment of its inception. Thus if the collective experience is now
one of impotence and a degeneration of idealism so advanced as to
make of idealism itself a synonym for naivety, paralleled by a collapse
of sexuality into abstention on the one hand and pornography on the
other, is it any wonder that *Uncle Vanya* is discovered to be occupying
such a prominent position in the classical oeuvre? It is tempered for the
time.

But if it is the fate of great texts to be employed in this unconscious
way as an element of social discipline, both reflecting social values but
also endorsing them, and consequently, *policing* them, they are nevertheless not immune to the innocent question – so often ruled out of
order, but always trembling on our lip 'did it have to be thus?' In other
words, did Vanya have to be Vanya? Or better still, did he have to be
Uncle Vanya? That this secret enquiry exists is a testament to the very
naturalism that Chekhov made his *métier*. One of the great pretensions
of naturalism was – and remains – its implicit honesty, its freedom from
ideology, its anti-philosophic and anti-political nature. Chekhov, pio-
neering this form in theatre, was able to write with startling ingenuous-
ness. 'The artist is not meant to be a judge of his characters and what
they say; his only job is to be an impartial witness.' In the same letter
he says, 'My only job is to be talented, that is, to know how to distinguish important from unimportant testimony ...' (Letter to Suvorin,
1888). The contradiction contained in these two statements lies at the
heart of the naturalistic debate. The very act of 'distinguishing' the life
of one from another marks the point at which ethics enters artistic
endeavour.

How many of us still believe – or possibly, dare to articulate the belief
– that art influences life? In the decayed ruins of a critical theatre, reel-
ing from the preposterous assumptions of enlightenment ideology, it is
rash even to attempt to penetrate the complex psychological maze
through which an audience, in its many parts, might respond to a text
and create meanings, let alone endorse an author or applaud the
actions of his characters. Yet every artistic undertaking implicates its

participants in the will to affect. If *Uncle Vanya* and the Chekhovian cannon as a whole makes repudiation its ethical character, the best that can be achieved from the performance of the existing text, if it is not to be rendered into a bloodless idyll spun between an unsexed man and a never-to-be-sexual woman – a perverse beauty shared by Sonya and Vanya – is to indict the audience with precisely the same lack of heroism as the characters – 'Are you not all Sonyas? Are you not all Vanyas?' But indicting the audience has always been the weakest option in the director's cabinet of tricks, for it precisely gratifies bourgeois taste with its appetite for a little castigation before dinner. The mirror of complicity has always been dangled above the stage, and will always earn the ready applause that comes from having ourselves revealed yet again as *guilty*. This is the cul-de-sac of English theatre practice. Rather than indulging in such ethical parlour-games, the way with *Uncle Vanya* might lie not with the director at all, but with the contemporary writer restoring to the experience of the text that peculiar anxiety that attends on a narrative which cannot be absorbed in shame or self-reproach, or above all, pity. Another Vanya, stripped of his avuncularity, might tell what is the price that must be paid to leave the room, rather than describing the melancholy of remaining in it. This price is egoism, cruelty, and eventually, solitude.

In transfiguring Vanya through the simple expedient of allowing him a solitary success, the melancholia of the entire play is subverted, for in both fiction and reality, no action that is completed does not entice another. In classic fashion, such autonomy that follows on the restoration of will to the protagonist – the assertion of desire – ruptures comedy with its intimate dependency on failure, and draws him into the tragic landscape whose wilderness, willingly entered, must bring solitude or death. Here the audience cannot take refuge in guilt or pity, and the naturalistic ethic ceases to exercise its fatal grip on the imagination. This abolition of collective conscience describes an adieu to the humanist theatre. It also offers an antidote to the moral torpor that clings to what has become – whatever its origins – a 'national' property ...

Love in the museum: the modern author and the antique text*

For all its apparent chaos, dislocation, fracture and repudiation of crit- ical discipline – all that represents itself as the phenomenon of post- modernism – contemporary culture is nevertheless driven by a number of restless imperatives – sleepless nights of intolerance – which affect it in its many seemingly diverse functions. The most frantic of these – now near to an authentic neurosis – is its loathing of the secret. For all its visible promiscuity, contemporary culture is puritanical in its hatred for the dark, the obscure, the unexplained, above all for the private, the enclosed, essentially for that which disdains justification, function, util- ity. Its slogans are relentlessly democratic, but its instincts are authori- tarian, even while it conceals these authoritarian impulses behind infinitely benign slogans. 'Accountability', 'access', 'the right to know', 'information technology', 'the public domain', 'scrutiny' and so on, are apparently unobjectionable elements in the construction of an open society, yet the odour of decay that clings to these clichéd phrases should indicate the subtle metamorphosis that attaches to all intellec- tual constructs, their tendency to become the instruments of an inqui- sition in a society that is no longer merely open but transparent.

The policing of this system – the more effective for being frequently critical of the police, themselves now a quaint relic of old regimes – is now the function of the media, whether in its journalistic, entertain- ment, or so-called informational modes, and its proselytizing view of itself as the representative of the interests of the people brings it directly into an ironic and sinister relation with the Committees of Terror of the French Revolution, bodies equally obsessive about the imperative need to eliminate all forms of secrecy and equally arrogant in their assuming the mantle of the popular will. This neurotic demand for the illumina- tion of all dark places – metaphorically akin to the night sky in modern cities, so ablaze with surveillance that the stars are no longer visible (are the stars not secrets, after all?) unites activities as seemingly diverse as

* Given as a paper at the University of Sheffield, 31st May 1996.

[171]

computerized information retrieval systems and the violating activities of junk journalists. All things must be known, from the sexual tastes of film stars and princes to the formula for carbon-dating a pharaoh's tomb. This deluge of information, which vastly exceeds the wildest ambitions of the eighteenth-century rationalists, bears no relation to truth, exists without any moral dimension, and constitutes a threat to the imagination – indeed, it suspects imagination as its mortal enemy, for imagination does not know itself, disdains to confess, and dies of self-knowledge, which is the reason for its perpetual rebirth. The secret, the obscure, the inaccessible, the inveterately private, once the domain of privilege, is now the refuge of all that wills resistance to the new order of absolute transparency, for art cannot account for itself nor justify itself in terms of either the market or the public good. By contrast, the rhetoric of access, with its false appeal to yet another category of human rights – the right to instant understanding – threatens to reduce culture to the status of medicine or aphrodisiac. If there is to be an art which articulates its resistance to the transparent society it will only be recognized in the darker spaces of a landscape otherwise bleached of colour by the dazzling lamps of contemporary interrogation. I would contend that this form is – precisely as it always was – that which steps out of the darkness only to invite its participants to be swallowed by it again, the greatest of all forms, which is tragedy ...

. I have provided this critical overview of contemporary culture as a description of an atmosphere, a climate of ideology, in which creative life must struggle for the remaining oxygen that enables it to breathe, for without understanding the fatal struggle that rages between transparency and obscurity we cannot understand tragedy itself – indeed, are in danger of losing even our memory of it – for tragedy is the illegitimate of all art forms, the most devastating to social orders and consequently, the most de-civilizing, the darkest and yet simultaneously the most life-affirming, for precisely by standing so close to the rim of the abyss it delivers expression to the inexpressible, and stages emotions the so-called open society finds it almost impossible to contemplate. Plato's violent repudiation of poetry and drama in the fifth century B.C. is merely the first ideological statement of this unending war that rages between order and imagination, and the contemporary world, with its entire moral will invested in the threadbare notions of universal human happiness, finds itself equally uncomfortable with an art form that leaps over the fences so carefully erected by therapists, media mechanics, and social workers. How else do we explain the

[172]

absence of tragedy from bulk media, from the ideological centres of culture like the national theatres, and the inevitable critical collusion that occurs at every cultural moment, and which vociferously denies that tragedy is even possible to perform in mass society? Nothing describes the national neurosis more perfectly than the deluge of comedy that now swamps the culture, for comedy, with its appeal to apparently-shared principles, drums up a solidarity which is all the more dubious for its shrill intensity, just as the triumph of the musical reminds us that sentimental lies are more credible when they come accompanied.

What we are witnessing in this closing of ranks among media mechanics, politicians and cultural critics is the familiar terror of moral speculation that characterized Athens after Socrates and enlightenment Europe during the bloodbath of public happiness known as the French revolution. When all must be known, when all must be accessible, unambiguous, essentially functional, what possible pretext can tragedy have for its own existence except to cause restless nights to otherwise contented citizens? The secret of tragedy – its inviolable secret – its terrible power of dislocation – lies in the forbidden knowledge that these citizens have a fatal susceptibility to instincts which are perfectly incompatible with collective discipline. Whilst it is possible to wring pity from the spectacle of the sad, the spectacle of the tragic penetrates beyond pity and achieves its effects in that place of irrationality which is also home to desire. For all that Aristotle attempted to create an aesthetic which placed tragedy safely within the bounds of social regulation, its seductive authority reaches always to the self-determining, the self-describing, and the erotic. It is the private, the occluded, to which it addresses its disruptive powers.

In speaking of the secret, its allure, and its simultaneous power to cause horror and revulsion in the transparent society, it becomes possible to identify the pleasures and dangers of the classical text, now consigned to the realms of cultural archaeology. If the ideology of transparency is one of instant communication, the great narratives of antiquity – almost entirely tragic in character – possess moral ambiguities which cannot be incorporated into the project of absolute enlightenment. Despite the politicization of the modern museum, its obsessive pursuit of the inter-active and the plethora of explanatory labels, stereophonic guiding, lighting rigs and the rest – the conversion of display into consumption and gratification, in effect the industrialization of the museum – it is possible to imagine artefacts and images to which a child might come with a relative innocence. Supposing for one moment of pure heresy, this child were not permitted to know at all, that *uninformed* he or she confronted objects and images whose resonances were not tuned by the educational impulses of others, but stood, naked and exposed to the power of a thing which was awesome and dare we say, beautiful? The confusion, pleasure, irrational desire, stimulated by such an encounter, is perhaps analogous to the relation in which we now stand to the antique text, whether Hebrew or Classical, and their iconographic representations, for these are now effectively cultural secrets.

These narratives remain dimly familiar to us – they are after all, the deep humus of the European soul – but how many of us are able to name them? If Christ on the Cross is the greatest of these, and the least likely to be consigned to the darker spaces of culture, its sado-masochistic undertones have ensured that its authentically tragic character has become obscured by contemporary ethics. What then, of the other great cruelties that distinguish this unilluminated gallery of European culture? The Dance of Salome? The Massacre of the Innocents? David and Bathsheba? Susannah and the Elders? And one to which I have felt a particular attraction, Judith and Holofernes? In all of these, the working and re-working of the narrative by subsequent generations of artists has resulted in the refining of the most significant visual gestures of all time, gestures which transcend one art form and lodge in others, not least between painting and sculpture and the tragic theatre. The shroud of secrecy that surrounds these profoundly disturbing images makes them powerfully desirable, the more so because there clings about them a transgressive moral atmosphere, something simultaneously forbidden and enticing.

It has been one of the many disastrous consequences of naturalism in the theatre that the idea of the contemporary has dominated subject matter to the exclusion of nearly every mythical, biblical or classical subject. By some profoundly false logic, it has been assumed that any artist concerned with the age in which he lives must mirror that age on the stage, must imitate the life of the street and reproduce its vocabulary. The poetic, the metaphoric, and the counter-suggestive have been largely sacrificed to the compulsion to speak effectively about what is misleadingly termed 'the real world'. The neurosis surrounding the relations between audiences and artists – the peculiar determination to create an ideology out of clarity and communication – means that the subject matter of the Hebrew or Classical world, let alone its moral implications – is now judged obscure and therefore barely legitimate. But the production of art is a half-blind process, a paradox whose quality arises not from control or absolute knowledge but from the friction of prejudice and perception. In lifting the mythical text from its obscurity, a contemporary author experiences some of the anxiety and ecstasy that accompanies the early stages of a love affair, for just as the power of the loved one resides in their potential to de-stabilize your life, so the antique text, so resonant with its mystery, its aura of interpretation, cannot yield itself up without a struggle, a struggle which may do permanent injury to a carefully-constructed life.

These are not after all, stories of the Humanist era, a fact which alone renders them profoundly suspicious to modern culture with its pretensions to having effectively abolished vengeance, rage, and even virtue in the interests of harmony. But to rescue the obscure text is not of course, to suffer any obligation to adopt a scholarly responsibility towards its content. One cannot but come to these great narratives with the eye and ear of one's own time, and just as every painting of the Crucifixion from Fra Angelico to Salvador Dali has brought into the frame not only the subject but the interpretative prejudice of its creator, so every re-telling on the stage or in literature encrusts the theme with further variations, and re-negotiates the moral dilemmas in the light of the modern.

I had myself seen a dozen or more representations of the Judith story – at least the crucial image of the beheading – before I considered reading the account in the Book of Judith in the Apocrypha. This account, consigned to the Apocrypha for its dubious moral implications, tells of a Jewish heroine who murders for political reasons a man she has seduced. It is on the surface, a narrative of heroism, nationalism, race-pride and self-sacrifice, profoundly significant elements which nevertheless seemed to me marginal to the psychological disturbance created by the subject – the lethal nature of sexual desire, the threat of annihilation that hovers about the margins of all passionate encounters. Certainly this element is not absent from the two greatest representations of the subject, those of Caravaggio and Artemesia Gentileschi. The beauty that Caravaggio lends to Judith is the beauty that destroys a powerful man, but as she brings down the sword her expression is full of the ambiguity of a misused instinct, it is in effect, profoundly secretive. As a dramatist whose medium – the stage – is infinitely refined for the exploration of the secret, the exposure of all that is contrary, the elucidation of the unspoken, I sensed in this story one of the great seductive arguments of Western culture, for my Judith, in her seducing of her enemy, is herself seduced – even by the fact of seduction itself – and thereby poses a catastrophic problem for her mentor, the servant, a shadowy figure in all paintings of the subject but here made an uncompromising ideologist whose relentless drilling of Judith suffocates her instincts long enough for the assassination to occur. The authority of desire over political discipline might not have been lost on the Hebrew chronicler of the Judith story, but his ambitions were not likely to have been diverted from the necessity to create a national myth. With the Renaissance – obsessive for sex and death – the theme was almost inevitably turned on its axis. In the long ages of the Enlightenment, the story is submerged, for the very irrationality that is the source of its power can only have made it repugnant to regimes of consciousness that sensed desire to be reactionary. It is in the obscurity of the museum that the tragedy that is Judith's can be exposed for a contemporary audience, for this text can be read as tragedy rather than as triumph, as moral suicide rather than heroic self-sacrifice. If the denial of instinct is a cause of madness, if the hyper-valuation of family and state over sexual love is deformity, Judith is indeed rendered insane by her actions. Following the murder of her lover, Judith loses the power of movement and is fixed to the floor in a state of catatonic horror. The political servant, desperate to escape with the trophy of the dead man's head, but also unwilling to leave the heroine behind – for Judith has already become a national property – can only offer the mundane compensations of domestic bliss in an effort to stimulate her mistress.

When at last Judith discovers the power to rise off the floor, her hatred compels her to punish and humiliate the servant, who endures it for her own political ends. It is however, only a passing relief for Judith. Hatred – a natural and necessary recourse when shame becomes intolerable, reverts to herself. She has trespassed not against society but against herself. She is alienated from her own body.

I find it hard to imagine a more perfect metaphor for the struggle that rages over the body – the private space – between the state and the individual, than this antique tale from a now obscure book. Its power, as I have tried to indicate, comes both from itself and from the re-working of it through generations of artists – its manipulation, age by age, to tell its suddenly revealed secrets. In a similar way, there is no more haunting and irritating narrative of the agony of the body – and I use the word irritating in a positive, anxious sense – than the story of Helen of Troy, which for all the deliberate neglect now attaching to classical culture – is infinitely the greatest epic of desire, just as the Last Supper is the greatest epic of solitude and suicide, in world literature.

The attractions of Homer's Iliad for different periods obviously reflect the condition of changing cultural moments – the Victorians were thoroughly familiar with it, and it is no coincidence that one of London's best known statues – the naked warrior at Marble Arch – is of Achilles, the paragon of physical courage and loyalty, a suitable hero for an imperial race, particularly if one is able to gloss over the fascinating imperfections of this profoundly childish but eminently masculine man. The shadow which has fallen across this text in the late twentieth century might be explained by a contemporary antipathy for those aspects of human nature that Homer chose to examine – cruelty, malice, the arbitrary nature of existence, the brutality of war and love, in essence all those tragic themes that the dominant ideology of humanism finds it impossible to digest. Above all perhaps, there lies at the heart of the Trojan War the appalling secret of the erotic … for it is Helen alone that accounts for the destruction of so many cities, and Helen alone who drives the Trojans to a collective suicide. Contemporary ideology, suffused with an inflexible materialism, can only shift uncomfortably at the spectacle of a ten-year war fought over the body of a single woman. So far have we travelled from the notion of the privileged, the blessed, the authentically aristocratic, and indeed, the sacrificial, that wars fought over beautiful women are incomprehensible while wars fought over petrol make perfect sense to us. The body is however, not so easily consigned to the domestic or the pornographic as contemporary culture would like us to believe. My own meditation on the character of Helen of Troy, *The Bite of the Night*, was not the first attempt to resuscitate Helen for a modern audience – she appears both in Marlowe and Goethe – but anyone writing in the late twentieth century must disentangle himself form the intellectual undergrowth of his time – so far as it is possible to do so – before addressing the essential conundrum of this text. Thus, my own text begins with a squabble between a recalcitrant student and his tutor over the relevance of classical studies in a modern university. This is a university incidentally, which has long since been abandoned as a result of insolvency, but which the stubborn Dr Savage refuses to quit. The student, Hogbin, appears at the tutorial with his usual studied indifference. A pathetic child of the age of materialism and rock music, Hogbin can only discuss the Trojan War in terms of the inert forces of production and

[177]

exchange ... Dr Savage's own child, soon to be abducted, witnesses this whilst playing ball in the ruins ...

Savage and Hogbin, an agonized duo until Hogbin expires of despair – literally the consequence of his being unable to exist with contradiction – visit Troy after its fall and live through most of the twelve subsequent cities built on its site, in each of which the now aged Helen continues to exercise a terrible fascination. Homer himself found nothing to interest himself in the ruins, but for a twentieth-century chronicler, living in the aftermath of the destruction of Dresden, Warsaw or Berlin, the layering of cultures has a keen resonance. In each of these new Troys, Helen's disruptive erotic influence is seized upon as the cause of social disharmony, and she is punished by each subsequent regime by losing her limbs, a literal physical reduction which, typical of bureaucracy and party, fails to grasp the crucial difference between beauty and eros.

It is of course, perfectly possible for an imaginative writer to invent metaphors of comparable density from the random events of his own time or from the depths of his own imagination. It is my contention however, that a culture that ceases to negotiate and re-negotiate its relations with the great metaphors of the past injures itself, that by consigning to the darkness all those narratives it finds unpalatable for reasons of social ideology, it delivers itself to a breathless neophilism that diminishes human experience. Francis Bacon's screaming popes are reflections on Velasquez. Britten's War Requiem is the seizure of a medieval form for a secular function. The great architectural ecstasies of European cities are the outcome of infinite refinements and repudiations. So in the field of tragedy, to love the antique text is not to be intimidated by it, but to invoke its authority for new purposes. Far from being a reactionary practice, to walk in the dark rooms of the antique is to feel – rather like a secret squeezing of one's hand by an illicit lover – powerful yet invisible allies in that devastating contest with new orthodoxies that characterizes the artistic life.

Creating a death*

Dancer, the protagonist of the play *Hated Nightfall*, is besieged by his own sensibility. He has perhaps the thinnest skin of any character I have invented – and thin skin is a painful condition at any time in the history of man. Our instinct from birth is to smother our delicate feelings in order to protect them from a climate of brutality, to develop those strategies of indifference that enable us to pass at a safe distance so much that would otherwise drive us mad. And Dancer has these strategies, which is why he frequently indulges a wilful cruelty, for the act of cruelty protects the one who inflicts pain on others from the terrible recognition of our mutual horror at the world's perpetual indifference. In Dancer the will to suicide, forever strong in him, encounters the social suicide of war and revolution. Revolution is rupture, violent as birth, to which it is often compared, but births are the creation of monsters as well as angels. The birth of Lenin's monster, simultaneously beautiful and instantly infected with the disease that will render it hideous, is a day-long glimpse of power for the tutor who has aspired to power all his life. Historical coincidence, material contradictions, the rash of ungoverned circumstance, lend this simmering soul an absolute authority which he chooses to deny from the outset, and rather than to enter History, to play with it, to make a toy of vast and mad machinery. And why? For perfect love.

Dancer's intellectual subtlety comes from the agonized condition of thin skin, for do we not feel lies long before we can rationally dissect them? The ideological is familiar to him. He knows the arguments too well, and can imitate their structures, even more effectively than those who honestly believe them. Thus his dancing skills, in skating and waltzing over the slogans of his enemies. Yet he is no reactionary. He no more credits the religion of the Tsars than the religions of the Bolsheviks. All argument is at his disposal. This is a man who might have

* First published as a note to the programme of *Hated Nightfall*, Royal Danish Theatre, 9th January 1997.

made a great career, at least until the inevitable collapse of cleverness before the arbitrary will of dictatorship. Yet he prefers the perfect sacrifice of one who, demonstrating his ability to own the world, casts all aside for the frail ecstasy of dying alongside those whom history has flung to the squalid grave of impotent ideas … Dancer's faith is precisely faith in nothing but faith itself … a final barrier against nihilism and the excruciating pain of knowing nothing but death is truth … Dancer's construction of a perfect death becomes, stage by stage, his vocation, and in its moment he is – paradoxically – relieved of his awful solitude, a solitude produced by excessive insight into those who surround him, the ugly, the beautiful, the unambitious and the fanatical.

If the twentieth century has been obsessed by History, this man is its antithesis. And he is not alone in this quality of evasion that is the private power of so many characters in my plays. In *The Power of the Dog* the Hungarian model Ilona finds a macabre pleasure in turning History into a mere stage for her own beauty, a tactic that cannot be tolerated for long. And in *Victory*, the widow Bradshaw reverses every ideal that has governed her life in a search for an accommodation with power that will lend her a little peace and possibly, love. Dancer is however, not a victim but a master, flung into higher places by the turning of the wheel. As his employers fall, he rises, and even supreme authority cannot touch him, at least so long as it remains at the far end of a telephone. Yet he has in the end no appetite for power. Its poverty is revealed to him even as he utters its oaths. The antithesis of a tragic hero of the Jacobean age, he does not sin for power, but repudiates it as it falls into his hands. For him, it is not enough, its laws are simple and once learned, cease to gratify. His fault is that of a plethora of knowledge, excessive vision that makes of all an agonizing transparency, even the melancholy pain of the priest-become-secret-policeman, with whom he shares a brief and pitiful bond. Dancer, suspended in life by an illusion, that of the perfectibility of desire, once permitted to examine it under an intimate gaze, finds it cannot be compared to something vastly more chilling and possibly ecstatic – the sacrifice. Offered the prospect of love in exile with the desired Empress, he knows he must pursue the harder goal … refusing her, he identifies it thus: 'I would lie with the silence of a spent lover and grieve under the seagulls for the apotheosis I had shirked …'

Dancer's repudiation of the twentieth century is a plea for a complexity of emotion, a form of tenderness that has been crushed by realpolitik and perverted Reason. In his last words reside a teacher's last advice, perhaps wasted on the air, to his loved but doomed pupils, simultaneously an adieu and a plea for something that has – perhaps temporarily – been abolished from the world.

The house of infection: theatre in the age of social hygiene*

Literally and metaphorically there is now no darkness in the world. Because nothing occurs in the moral sphere without the appearance of a corresponding material phenomenon, we can say that just as we have drowned the secret of the stars in the floodlights of our cities, so we have blinded ourselves in the dazzling scrutiny of transparency and interrogation. The open society is white and bright. It abhors the shadows. It violates the penumbra of privacy in the name of access. It trespasses in the most secret chambers of grief and makes advertisements of pain. It transforms all experience into news and subjects all instinct to the spurious discipline of debate. Absolute light. Light as a system. Light as a *regime*.

The first policeman carried a lantern. Only later was he given a sword. From Genesis onwards European culture aspired to illumination. Light shone from the eyes of kings and later it became the substance of democracy. They talked of light in the eighteenth century as if it were synonymous with air, with breath, with health. Enlightenment was their word. Dark corners were unhealthy, sewers or drains. Dark rooms could only harbour conspiracies, of the aristocracy, of the church. Liars preferred the dark. And the streets became dazzling, not only to banish crime, but as an aspiration, as a triumph over night.

And still today we use figures of speech associated with the simple antithesis of light and shade. We talk of 'throwing light' on a subject which has become obscure, as if somehow the lifting of a blind would show all complexity was chimerical. We use the phrase 'the light of day' as an oath to banish evasion or deceit. We know the vampire perishes with the sunrise. Light always betokens truth, and as it was the dream of prisoners, so it has become the narcotic of democracy, simultaneously the ecstasy of the police and the entitlement of the press, a license to violate. We live the culture of Absolute Illumination, the questioning of which can only invite the familiar and brutal riposte 'So what do

* Given as a paper at the University of Dresden, 1st October 1996.

[182]

you have to conceal?' mouthed no longer by the secret police, a quaint relic of primitive surveillance, but by the universal journalist.

And now we must announce the very terminus of all obscurity, the officially sanctioned obliteration of the final secret. The Church of Rome has embraced total transparency. Henceforward, its confession boxes will be made of glass. Penitence in private bears the odour of deceit, so every shame will be confessed before the crowd, a reform so profound as to stand alone as testimony to the triumph of scrutiny, whilst at the same time admitting the never-absent instinct in all of us to *perform* our grief before an audience and to make of this historic and dark transaction the subtle and contemporary discipline called – a *game show* ...

Now we see the apotheosis of democracy to be mutual surveillance, at its worst pornography, at its most deceptively benign, investigative journalism, let us proceed to examine the way in which the artist can be implicated in the Illumination System, at least as far as theatre is concerned. Let us look again to the phrase – so stale and dead-in-the-mouth as to be instantly redolent of utter decay in its content value – 'to throw light on' – this throwing of light being intended to initiate debate around an issue of 'public interest', which – in populist culture – means anything at all, since the distinction between private and public has been actively dissolved. The urge to participate in 'light throwing' is something to which few artists are immune, indeed it is a time-honoured instinct among dramatists with a pedigree reaching far beyond the great illuminators, Brecht and Shaw. Who, on first consideration, could quarrel with the proposition that theatre might be employed to improve the circumstances of our lives, that it might encourage rational consideration of issues of significance in society, that it possesses the potential to be every bit as utilitarian as a lecture, or under extreme circumstances, a stone? The theatre of light will be theatre of critique, by definition it must *reveal* ... this revelation being – as with all exposure – only the pretext for judgement. Whereas under certain cultural systems the throwing of light has the potential to produce instant scandal and even potential political intervention, in the blazing forum of the Illumination System, the exposure/judgement cycle has become no more than an element in the entertainment programme, and critical theatre consequently an aspect of the boulevard miasma.

Since nothing is immune from the perspiring athleticism of an ideology, the abhorrence of the dark that characterized all Brecht's practise

[183]

has become – as with so much that once was owned by communism – the new slogan of a dying democracy, the stiff and rusting mechanism of old Stalinist bureaucracies imported wholesale by the West to advertize its infatuation with all that's popular and cheap to buy. Brecht advocated a bright auditorium, precisely in order to compel the critical stare that makes for mutual surveillance. And since actors only appear mysterious by virtue of the dark, these agents of truth must also be revealed as no more than speakers of ideas, stripped of the autonomy they had historically enjoyed. Darkness seemed to Brecht a relic of tragedy, the habit of obscure despotism. Reason and critique flourish in states of white light, and darkness harbours delinquency, the private, the impossible to discipline.

The bright theatre of our time, so critical as to be the favoured form of national companies, so revealing as to be not merely morally perfect but commercial – repudiates above all that which is *obscure*, lightless, morally confused. Our national theatres are palaces of light, the foyer itself a dazzling antechamber to the intellectual enlightenment that must follow the opening of the doors ... and this experience will be first and foremost a *telling*. The contemporary theatre text as authorized by the national institutions of theatre is primarily an article of revelation, and consequently, dramatized information, the pretext for that sterile transaction which sends the audience away into an illuminated night full of the gratification of sharing an easily-digested truth – a truth which is essentially, *transparent*. Just as, in the early days of public hygiene, children considered to be under the average weight were, for their own protection, exposed to a barrage of sunray treatment, so the modern audience is ranked in rows before the glare of relentlessly harmonious light-sources, unambiguous truths designed to stimulate a preposterous solidarity. The writers of the critical theatre are the low technicians of the Illuminated Society.

This dazzled culture which has ceased to study the firmament despises imagination equally. It requires of art that it is – *lucid*. And if the text is to be lucid, the production must make its first ambition – *clarity*. And these are the words not of a malcontent, but of the critical police, who applaud these virtues to the skies, lending them a status far beyond the essentially unstable quality of beauty. For them, clarity *is* beauty, for them what is clear *is* beautiful. And the beauty of this clarity consists in the elimination of the unhealthy state of not-knowing. Not-knowing, a state if not of darkness, then of a lingering on darkness's rim, a purgatory of the penumbra, is now to be experienced as sickness. No longer is there some quaint charm in ignorance, a nobility in remoteness from fixed truths. Light as the cultural and spiritual determinant demands that no solitary individual remains outside the access syndrome. In populist democracy, the criminal concept is that of the *elite*, and in order that no visible elite shall declare itself, information must be public, gratis, and even – we are near now to the final solution – *obligatory*. We shall not only pity the unknowing – a Victorian sentiment of peculiar fragility – we shall insist on their elimination. The new poverty is to be *without information*, to be disconnected from the light.

We have noted that under late democratic populist societies, we endure critique as a social music, a clamorous accompaniment to the Illumination System, repetitive, regimented as the beat of rock music, itself a domesticated spasm of social resentment. We have observed further that those artists blithely posturing in the garments of dissidence in the contexts of the national theatre system are incorporated into the culture of transparency, propped into position by aesthetic prejudices like clarity or lucidity. We have described how it is precisely the provision of an inexhaustible diet of critical realism that lubricates the populist system, itself governed by a media that makes grievance and telling a mild erotica, a pornography. In this climate of perpetual and obsessive health, a clinic of endless diagnosis and prognostication (itself now narcotic just as the surgery is a place of pilgrimage for the unadored), what is the prospect for a theatre of imagination? When social hygienic and collective harmony have become – not the aspiration of injured solitude but a regimentation and a Utopian discipline, in effect a drill performed both in and outside the theatre – what is the shape of the authentically dissident text?

If a serious theory of dramatic practice is to exist it can only do so on the basis of an analysis of social formation. If the dominant power of our period is information technology, absolute access to information, and social transparency at every level of experience, dramatic practice must pose *knowledge* against information, *speculation* against journalism, *imagination* against evidence. This is to say, it must re-enter the darkness from which it emerged. This darkness is primarily an absence. Just as the darkness of the night was created precisely by the absence of illumination, so this theatre that aspires to darkness is without lucidity, clarity or utility. Health and light – the double intention of all critical theatre – are replaced by the infectious secret of the single form which, taking darkness as its essential quality, is the nausea of all political and post-political systems – tragedy.

[185]

Let us talk of tragedy, for it is the greatest of all art forms and the most beautiful, and for these reasons alone almost abolished by the Illumination System, hating beauty as it must and afraid of the dark as an aged bachelor shudders at the shadow on his door. This is a society of the timid which, even whilst it licenses every violent act and every shape of fornication in the name of liberty, still has a horror of autonomy. Populist democracy can tolerate very little of the active self, for self is no respecter of rights, and tragedy is the supreme moment of self and the worst enemy of rights, it tramples rights, it is after all is said and done, the *illegal form of things*. Is there a single tragic protagonist who could not be described prima facie, as one who murders rights? Tragedy is not humanist and intends no good to man. But intending no good to him, it enhances him. That is its mystery and precisely its power to unsettle the soul.

When critique is not only the licensed form of dramatic practice, but an obligation, the profoundly *uncritical* nature of a tragic theatre renders it an object of suspicion and contempt. For its chosen discourse is not one of transparency. Contrary to the first rule of the humanist theatre – be lucid – its very language is obscure, opaque, diversionary, complex, irreducible, indeed, a poetry, and poetry is the furthest of all intellectual practice from information, it mocks information, it exiles information to the margins of human experience. It is unnecessary to say that no tragedy depends on research, nor does it require a single fact for its substantiation. It is also incompatible with any political programme, it advances no cause and therefore declines to descend into the market place of competing ideologies, a novel offence in a society where the cacophony of party debate is discerned as a sign of health. And darker still, it communicates nothing but pain. The sound of the lazar house. And pain is the exclamation of ill-health, the abolition of which is the pretext of all social and political action, the goal of the harmony programme. All political parties and opinion manufacturers, of whatever colour, are dedicated to the *elimination of pain*. And tragedy declares pain is not only inevitable, it calls it *necessary*. It makes pain its subject, it makes a passion of pain. This pain is, furthermore, without political solution. It is without relief other than the relief of death, and so far removed, therefore, from the utilitarian function of critical drama, as to be strictly incompatible with social life.

This is the darkness – the quality of darkness – which the Illumination System might well be satisfied to leave alone, for such absolute obscurity seems unlikely to draw an audience within its unlit portals –

and they shall be unlit, in contrast to the blazing foyer of the national institutes. But they have not forgotten the lure of ill-health. The enduring fact is this – the spectacle of pain, rendered in poetry – is aphrodisiac …!

One of the claims to new authority exercised by the Illumination System is its sexual visibility. Here also, nothing is permitted to remain unrevealed. The pornographic is revelation on a single plane, the screen, the page. Rape is the violation of the private dark, a growing phenomenon of the Access culture, for shall we not have access to each other, and is not permission an archaism, a statement of unforgivable privacy? So much sex, and so little that is erotic, for the erotic is a pain, a pain of contemplation whose beauty is essentially tragic, an aspiration beyond the capacity of the physical to satisfy. This is knowledge, and not information. It has as much in common with the access society as a lover's suicide has in common with the anatomical drawing of a womb …

If the power of tragedy – of darkness – lies in the poetic articulation of incurable pain, if it is the lyrical expression of the lazar house, it possesses almost by definition, the power to communicate itself as a disease is transmitted, hand to hand. It is an infection, and this quality of infection finds its origin in an individual who historically and culturally has been the captain of the ship of fools – the actor. The tragic theatre is an actor's theatre as the critical theatre is its antithesis, annihilating the actor, calling his practice a mere discipline, a mechanical activity whose artifice must be *observed* – or in more contemporary versions, the actor ceases to exist at all – the public becomes its own performer, invited to initiate drama on its own. Just as the reformation decried the priest, so public theatre of a certain kind despises the actor. In *tragedy* he is – she is – by contrast, revered, he or she is characterized by an expertise which is the necessary foundation for an inspiration, primarily a voice whose cadences can register the extremities of pain and make pain beautiful. It is the actor who is placed at the heart of tragic experience and in the ecstasy of performance communicates in a language specific to the tragic stage, therefore a secret, a privilege and inaccessible, intractable and irreducible. No tragic language can be annexed by the information and broadcast system. It is incompatible with mass dissemination. Its sickness renders it horrible to the light of small-screen day …

Against illumination, debate and critique, tragedy offers darkness, the spectacle of pain which is politically insoluble, a new language, and

[187]

the instrument of special articulation, the actor. All tragedy is unhealthy, all tragedy repudiates the dominant concept of social uniformity. It replaces it with the spectacle of violent dissent and it enacts it in the unregulated interstices of the dominant culture. But if a theatre of infection becomes at certain moments a necessity of the human psyche in the same way that disease is a necessity of the species – disease in the body being a paradigm for the absolute imperfectibility of human experience – how does an audience recognize its organic aspiration, its special aptitude for ill-health? For are we not discussing here – in the identification of tragedy as a malevolent practice – an appetite, an inclination for sickness?

The Illuminated Society incorporates all artistic practice into the utility programme. The critical police, operating at the highest levels of the culture, ratchet up the harmonious orchestra of comedy and social critique. Every subject that is not a comedy is a problem. As we have discussed above, the revelation, discussion and solution of problems has become the approved function of art. Scandals of public life, the squalor of the drug addict, criminality, depravity among the dispossessed, all such subjects belong safely within the system we have identified, never testing the conscience, the condition of which can be relied upon as *absolute conviction*, a flaccid drumskin against which every glancing blow will reverberate in a predicted way ...

It is, therefore, the suicide of the conscience that is held out by the Theatre of Infection as its claim on the imagination, nothing less. The critical theatre presents its audience with no ordeal. If it created a conscience, it now plays it as an instrument whose strings however slack, however poorly tuned, can still be relied upon to resonate to platitudes and familiar themes. It is this dying music that fills our halls of culture. These melancholy tones are the accompaniment to the Illumination System and the background to the moral transactions of the contemporary stage. Therefore, *the ordeal of the audience* must be the first intention of the tragic theatre and the howling sound of breaking and strained strings its first polyphony. We do not insult the audience. We do not pretend to own a superior metaphysics. We do not provoke it to anger, or humiliate it for its demographic origins. We do not put it under light or offend it by scrutiny. And our darkness extends to the foyer which must possess the quality of calm and tranquillity, the proper preparation for the coming experience of moral agony, endured at the hands of actors for whom this performance will be sacred trust. By contrast, the racket of the theatre foyer in the society of access and illumination, its commercialization of the preparation for the experience of art, its alcohol, its muzak, its bookstands, its lottery stall, is contrived degeneration, the sham democratic odour of entertainment. In the House of Infection the audience attends in the only condition possible for the experience of tragedy – *anxiety*. This anxiety arises from the profound apprehension as to the fate of its conscience – the diametrically opposite condition from that experienced on entering the Illuminated Theatre where laughter, the exchange of anecdotes, news, gossip, reveal relief that nothing can occur which might damage the fragile peace of mind created by collective conscience and its well-known melodies ...

The essential character of tragedy – its invitation to a suicide of conscience within the dark space of privileged time – makes it an act of secession in contemporary culture, for it evades surveillance by the nature of its ambiguities. In a benign regimentation of things according to the realist aesthetic, information substitutes itself for knowledge, mimesis for truth. Here it is the abolition of information that licenses the imaginative excess of tragedy, the discarding of all imitation that permits its challenge to contemporary reality ...

It is unwise to think that a laughing audience – unanimous and gratified by skill and competence in production – does not harbour an unarticulated sense of lack, an absence. This lies low ... the vestiges of a mutiny ... The intensification of the Illumination System serves only to heighten this obscure sense that sickness is – in the artistic sphere as in the body – a potential axis of perception ... more even, a *desire*. From this secret, from this confession of the profoundest strata of unviolated privacy, a new practice might be conceived. Without it, theatre is condemned to repeat, ever less convincingly – since the actor's voice betrays what his intelligence cannot grasp – the slogans of a morally hygienic culture.

The Play of Seven Days

A play was written lasting seven days
Its length alone ensured no dramaturg no play-surgeon no agent no
producer no manager no publisher would even turn the title page
Therefore the Play of Seven Days was immune to every prejudice
except one and could be performed only by those who believed theatre
was a place

> Without laws
> Without duties
> Without obligations to the
> well-being of the public
> Its tolerance
> Its tempers
> Its fatigues

In other words only by those for whom Art was a prejudice
And these together made the Play of Seven Days
Made it for no one at all
And her who was no part of an equation

> No element of a deal
> Not in need of education
> Had read the whole of literature and still cried
> Hearing the rumour of its existence
> (The Play of Seven Days being necessarily a rumour)
> Came
> And sat unearthly still
> And at the end of seven days declared
> The play promised more than it delivered
> Such themes surely required the abolition of all
> compromise?
> In the meantime she waited impatiently for
> The Play of an Entire Year

Part II

A dialogue with David Ian Rabey

Rabey. Lvov's assertion in *The Last Supper*, 'Only catastrophe can keep us clean', echoes Bianca's line 'Catastrophe is also birth' in *Women Beware Women*, and Starhemberg's forcible tuition of Concilia in *The Europeans*. One definition of catastrophe is the experience of living beyond the point where death is preferable to continued existence, and I wonder how close this is to your own sense of catastrophe as potential explosion of spurious notions of life's worth or purpose, opening up tormenting roads to liberation. Your characters discover capacities to perform realignments in their selves through catastrophe which are incredible even to them, the phenomenon described by Helen in *The Bite of the Night* as the human ability to lose one's mind and yet find others, to lose one's sight yet see through other channels; and these characters are purposefully disturbing in begging the question as to how self-conscious or self-aware they are in their compulsions to excavate, explicate and perform their selves.

Barker. Catastrophe in my theatre is willed, as opposed to simply endured. Bradshaw's horror at her husband's quartering is only the beginning of a journey she undertakes. Her pain is a door to catastrophic experience, which she wills upon herself, almost as if she wished to expose herself to the whole range of possible disaster, and like a piece of wood or linen, to accept the warping which hostility inflicts on her. But the fullest manifestation of catastrophe occurs in the choice Savage makes in Act I Scene I of *The Bite of the Night*, the discarding of family, the passage of sacred barriers which inhibit knowledge. This is a rupture which is made in isolation from the external. His wife, on the other hand, seizes a catastrophic opportunity with the fall of Troy to deliberately lose herself. And others also interpret bad fortune as a concealed escape, for example, Bianca's reluctant acknowledgement of meanings attaching to her own ordeal, and a forced examination of her own sexual nature. And in *Brutopia* Cecilia exposes herself to the risks of insanity or violent

[193]

death in her ruthless relationship with Henry VIII. What lies behind the idea of catastrophe is the sense of other varieties of the self repressed or obscured by politics, social convention, or simple fear. Bradshaw's journey is ostensibly one of piety – the collecting of her husband's parts – but it leads to acts of outrageous impiety. Savage commits impious acts as the condition of his tour. The will to be whole, and perhaps more than whole, is discovered in opposition to collective sentiment. Dramatically, the technique for summoning the will for this act of persistent rupture consists in constant self-description, the exhortation which found its first expression in a rudimentary form in Billy McPhee's last words in *That Good Between Us*.

Rabey. The most compulsive characters in your recent plays – *Women Beware Women*, *The Bite of the Night*, *The Europeans*, and *The Last Supper* – are self-appointed liberators who consciously inflict pain to stimulate. Is the willing of catastrophe on self and others the same as the impulse to tragedy?

Barker. The tragic resides in the refusal of the individual to leave the personality unexcavated, the eruption of will into areas of social piety. Savage's painful expression of secret thought, and the act contingent upon it, bring both him and Helen into the tragic arena. On the other hand conventional tragedy demands punishment for transgression – mental disorder or death. It is the revenge of the collective upon the savage ego. Savage is not punished, at least not by the collective, and Starhemberg defies the collective to the end, drawing Katrin with him. So these plays are not tragic but catastrophist. The tragic dénouement, the restoration of discipline over self by society or deity, seems to be in Shakespeare a neutered thing, a watery agency without vigour, unfelt and unbelieved. The punishment Savage receives is terrible loneliness, the effect of knowing too much. Starhemberg and Katrin discover new life through a love that can only be discovered in the extreme of resistance. As with Livia and Leantio, their claim on each other is conditional on rejection of reconciliation with the state. Lvov dies, but then he wishes to.

Rabey. A recurrent theme in your work is the body, its mutilation and forcible mutation by self and others; Helen wonders 'What joint or knuckle, what pared-down shredded section would be the point at which your love would say stop, *essential Helen*?' The drive to discover how much can be done to the human body before it ceases to be desirable, talismanic or powerful emerges as unsettlingly vital. The transgression of ostensible physical limitations and ideals breaks, by association, conventional socially restrictive notions of beauty, desirability, and endurance. For example, in *The Europeans* Starhemberg's ruthless adoration of Katrin leads him into rebellion against the aesthetic ideal of beauty which sends shockwaves into the State's ideal of order.

Barker. The body as conventional ground for controlled desire is one of the undeclared cornerstones of the State. It is inevitably associated with youth, especially with fertility, and effectively locates sexual charisma at the shallowest point. The freedom that some of my characters discover in locating sexual power in the frame of experience, e.g. pain, relates desire to the interior life rather than in the skin-deep fascination of the icon. Helen of Troy is described by Homer and all who follow him as youthful, beautiful, impossible-to-see-without-desire, etc., and Helen herself as reluctant, the victim of her appearance, and so on. But we know beauty has nothing to do with desire, and that a beautiful woman cannot launch a thousand ships, whereas we suspect a desirable woman might. This distinction is at the crux of *The Bite of the Night*. The state depends for its continuation on the cult of family and fertility, and fetishizes it by its collusions with the propagation of the beautiful, as thing to be possessed, as body owned and sold. I emphasized this in *Women Beware Women*, but also showed Sordido's ravishing of Bianca as the reverse of the coin. In *The Europeans* Katrin's atrocious condition is a spur to desire in Starhemberg, her eroticism lying precisely in her impossible-to-assimilate history. She has none of the functions of fertility, being unable to feed an infant. By loving Katrin Starhemberg publicly breaks the silent contract of socialized love.

But the body as locus of abuse and fetishization goes back earlier than these plays, certainly to *The Love of a Good Man*. The state has always played fictional games with the flesh of the dead. The Unknown Warrior is a response to the phenomenon of incomprehensible slaughter in the twentieth century, and designed to be an anonymous representation of sacrifice. In other words, the annexation of the innocent for the purposes of the State. I examined this proposition from a number of angles in the play. The symbolic and the actual coincide in the games played around the identity of a single corpse in the midst of monumental mourning. On the other hand, the State's ferocious dismembering of its enemies is of course the motor to *Victory*. The personal ache to recover the murdered, euphemistically called 'The fallen' in the Great Wars, but the 'criminal' after Great Revolutions, reaches its apotheosis in Bradshaw's theft of her husband's head from the sleeping monarch, who transports it about with him, a more powerful talisman than the works hatched inside it. This hypnosis induced by the presence of the body defies rationalism, as we can see in the supreme obscenity of Lenin's tomb. While you are a useful pretext for social policy your body is mummified. As soon as you are discredited, your remains are attacked. Stalin was turfed out of his mausoleum. His flesh had to be abused as well as his ideas. And this in the super-rational society.

Rabey. *Women Beware Women* and *The Europeans* depict speculative, disruptive actions which defy the sentimentalities of false democracies; these actions attack the ideal of 'kindness' by which populism discourages completeness of the self and the individual's will to know the true nature of his or her desires.

Barker. I have tried to open the idea of kindness to examination because it is so frequently employed as a ban on action, a means of stifling will and self-expression. There is a form of kindness which is nothing to do with 'kind' at all, but is a relentless charity which distorts the nature of the doer. Thus to be kind to one's relatives might be to stunt oneself, to be kind to the weak might stunt the ability of the weak to develop their own strategy and so on. Kindness becomes a form of oppression, enabling us to refuse courses of action on the grounds they might injure others. Against this regime of delicacy, Livia's ruthless setting of Sordido on Bianca in *Women Beware Women*, and Starhemberg's despatch of Concilia in *The Europeans*, are acts of calculated violence which are creative to both the perpetrator and the ostensible victim. I have tried in *Brutopia* to look for a creative form of kindness in the person of Cecilia. She looks for a truthful form of it, declaring she cannot find kindness in the company of the kind, knowing as she does her father's kindness to be the fake virtue of a Renaissance egotist. More was, in his political relations, a most unkind man, vituperative and merciless, whose Utopia is socialized oppression based on sexual abstinence.

Rabey. In *The Last Supper*, Lvov is an incarnate offence to populism in his completeness of self, when populism promises the provision of so-called 'essential' complementary elements and contexts which prove to be debilitating, intoxicating and addictive. I'm reminded of Nietzsche's identification of the herd instinct and its enshrined apotheosis in religion. You also seem fascinated by the promises and images of religious faith.

Barker. Lvov creates a religion out of denial, insisting always on returning responsibility to the individual seeker. He is never placatory and rarely congratulatory, making independence of self the first condition of freedom. He plays two versions of kindness against each other, knowing that only by repression are we able to perform acts of social kindness, whereas only by acts of self-affirmation do we achieve the other sorts of kindness, truth to character. The persistent acts of rupture he performs with public morality entail an isolation from alternative sources of power. It is paramount for Lvov that he will not play the messiah to those seeking simple moral consolations; the officer asks for a pacifist lecture and goes away empty-handed, as does the farmer, a sinner whose sin we never learn. At the end of the play, the returning officer, hardened and revolutionary, declares that those will be punished who did not make their messages clear – the first priority of power being the unambiguous repetition of moral postures.

I am less interested in writing exposures of religion than in describing the constant swing between submission and independence that religion generates. Sloman, after attacking Lvov for his refusal of democracy, cannot resist the man's sheer self-assertiveness, which he finds immaculate, and after a collective act of cannibalism it is he who asserts the unity of all who have participated. It is Sloman who is the potential high-priest of the cult. Thus his 'Hold Hands!' is both a cry of solidarity but also of mutual enslavement. The accommodation which the individual is prepared to make to sustain faith is inordinate, a kind of longing for servitude of mind, and this can be observed in the great rationalist religions also. When Gisela is brutally exposed to bad sex by Lvov, an attempt to break her loyalty, she manages to turn her very proper anger into a controlling pity for him, and it is a source of bitter frustration to him that he cannot break their will to servitude. But the best religious figures are those who are essentially corrupt, and know their corruption. As Stucley declares in *The Castle*, what help can the perfect be to the imperfect? Only the imperfect can help the imperfect.

Rabey. Whereas populism seeks to impose restrictive definitions of the self, the polar opposite force might be desire, which challenges even the *self-defined* limits of the self in a surge of derationalizing intuitive legitimacy, a liberation available to all yet defying generalization.

Barker. Passion destabilizes the character, and by extension, the social cohesiveness of the polity. It is literally incapacitating, which was why it has been regarded as an infliction or a sickness. But desire, reciprocated, directs energy and makes transformation both internal and external. Thus Ann and Skinner together can move mountains (*The Castle*) but Skinner alone becomes a monument to defiance, strenuously powered and a subject of desire in herself, who has no access to desire any more. The cult of Skinner and her wound, her terrible absence, lends her the prospect of real political power, but it is a sterile thing compared to her original state. On the other hand, there is something condemned about Ann's hunger for Krak, and his own dissolution in it. It is unequal and ill-fitting, and its cruelties are not creative in the way that say, Starhemberg's are in *The Europeans*. In all the relationships of desire in my work up until *The Bite of the Night* there is a stronger and a weaker element, whether it's Ann's weakness vis-a-vis Skinner or Leantio's vis-a-vis Livia. But between Helen and Savage there is a relentless and ferocious drive that finds a mutual inspiration, an inevitable passage of destruction.

Rabey. It strikes me that impulses to severance are crucial to your work – demanding the courage to act on one's love or hatred, or, most disturbingly, one's inextricably mingled love *and* hatred.

Barker. 'Impulses to severance' is a good phrase, raising once again the spectre of self-inflicted pain as a means to new knowledge, and yes, the hurt done to a loved one – and by extension, to oneself – is the supremely catastrophic example. This is difficult to articulate. It is near to the subject that occupies much of my attention as a writer, the nature of the bad spirit, the meaning of wickedness. The rupturing of conventional pieties is a common theme in my work – Savage's murder of his father in *The Bite* (it is technically a suicide, but Savage demands it), Orphuls's killing of his mother in *The Europeans*, Cecilia's ecstasy in her father's death in *Brutopia*, all of them gateways to self-development but also appalling and traumatic. There is an earlier form of this in Bradshaw's conscious dehumaniza-tion of her son in *Victory*. What the characters do in rupturing these bonds is to create morality for themselves, as if from scratch. They insist on a carte blanche, however impossible. It is as if they were seeing their own lives as theatre, and demanding the right to invent themselves.

Rabey. The simultaneous co-existence of love and cruelty, or desire and pain, in your work is a more complex theme than can be encapsulated in the simplistic terms of deviancy, 'sadism' and 'masochism', in which social notions of deviance have their own effects of oppressive cultural (non-) legitimization. Lvov describes love as 'doing the undoable.' How might we distinguish love from desire?

Barker. To take the first part, you are correct to expose terms such as 'sadism' and 'masochism' as attempts to bolster a spurious normality in sexual relations. Not all acts of cruelty between lovers can be interpreted as sadism unless a real hatred of the other, as opposed to the profound resentment that lies at the root of desire, is the source of it. By resentment I intend this – the anger, and even shame, felt by the partner in the presence of the inextinguishable power of the other's sex – the spectacle of endless servitude (and ecstasy is a servitude) that sexual power (i.e. sexual difference) lays before us. This is a landscape of hunger which (like cunt in Krak's futile drawings) has neither edge nor width, and forever entails the abolition of dignity and even self-knowledge in the birth and rebirth of wanting. This resentment at servitude lies in the heart of wanting itself, and produces the ambiguous sense of despair and fascination which might lead to violence, a violence shared by both parties. Now, this is nothing at all to do with De Sade's monotonous savagery, where the orgasm is the single end of all imagination, and the attainment of orgasm an ever-diminishing prospect, available only by further refinements of cruelty. De Sade's violence is never mutual – it is not shared pain, but infliction.

The word love is not uncommon in my work, but I only edged towards a meaning for it in *The Europeans*, which is subtitled '*Struggles to love*'. And here it is in many ways not mediated through the body as desire is. What Starhemberg does for – and also against – Katrin is to insist on her right to self-description, resistant to the categories invented for her by the state and refusing the false reconciliations of History on the one hand, or parenthood on the other. His love for her is a love for her completion, her pursuit, which he perceives and perhaps judges more finely than she does herself. This certainly involves 'doing the undoable'.

Rabey. The Power of the Dog's subtitle, 'Moments in History and anti-History', seems your first step towards identifying a mythic power in individual pasts as opposed to national pasts. This power is increasingly identified with sexuality in your work, particularly in *Women Beware Women* and *The Breath of the Crowd*, which highlight exposure and realization of the unlived life, the uniqueness of each personal testimony and the sense of cumulative power involved in sexual encounters.

Barker. There is little or no aperture in *The Power of the Dog* for celebration or the catalogue of restorative things that are commonly associated with the humanist theatre. But what it does assert is the capacity of individuals for alternative experience and private history, which both dives under and is swamped by collective politics. In a world of Historical Method, blunderingly performed by Stalin with materialist rhetoric, an alternative fetishism is created by the dis-located, a viable private madness in collective madness. The image of Ilona, fashion model and atrocity-addict, is not easily prised open by psychological or political interpretation. She is a self-invention of the historical moment, absurd and yet powerfully evocative of wrong-rightness. In this, the play prefigures *The Possibilities*, which are all approaches to the idea of wrong-rightness. They are amoral plays, but powerful assertions of human imagination at the moment when reconciliation is a greater disaster than extinction itself. The willed creation of private history (Ilona's collection of photographs), its resistance to world-historical forces (an appalling category if there ever was one), and its insistence on private perception at all costs (she will continue with her narcissism no matter what the objective conditions) come yet more defiantly in *The Europeans* where atrocity itself, as personified in Katrin, refuses to submit to absorption into historical material (the dead, the executed, the unknown warrior, the fallen, etc.) Katrin is the Screaming Exhibit, a phenomenon that rocks the Museum of Reconciliation. In all these plays, and, as you indicate, in *The Breath of the Crowd*, sexual history is made between characters with an authenticity that cannot distinguish their political actions. The dignity that is discovered in this struggle even lends a quality of beauty to the otherwise wholly disreputable. I'm thinking of Scadding in *Downchild*, for example.

Rabey. Your characters insist on absolute truthfulness, in self and others, in sexual relations, however harrowing the consequences. For example, Skinner in *The Castle* tells Ann to leave nothing out of her description of her relations with Krak, 'If I know all I can struggle with it, I can wrestle it to death . . .' Thus Skinner seeks relief from the self-torturing fascination of 'the imagined thing', which gnaws her to madness.

Barker. The demand for absolute truth in the sexual relationship is simultaneously the key to Skinner's evaluation to semi-divine status and a kind of emotional death. The truth is the devastation of hope. In a state of hopelessness she acquires the will to catastrophic experience, passing from passionate love-life to adamantine stoicism. As long as Ann remained untruthful, the possibility of reconciliation existed, though as a sort of half-life, the wanting in pursuit of the unwanting. But by submerging herself in scalding pain (the very last detail of infidelity), Skinner sheds a defunct self, a dead skin, and even seems to regard sexual madness as nearly comic, when Krak exposes his loss of self to her, his bewilderment in the state of passion.

Rabey. *Don't Exaggerate*, a direct address to the audience, seems a crucial development in locating obligation in the theatre audience on the specific occasion of performance. The prologues of *The Bite of the Night* and *The Last Supper* similarly emphasize the importance of what the witnesses choose to bring to, and give to, the theatrical experience.

Barker. The importance of *Don't Exaggerate* in my theory of theatre lay in its employment of contradiction and digression as means of returning the onus of moral decision to the audience. I now believe in the de-thronement of the audience, the abolition of its judgemental character, and the assertion of the stage over the auditorium. By this I mean the restitution of power to the actor, not as demonstrator of a given thesis, but as the figure who encourages the audience to abandon its moral and intellectual baggage and permit itself the greater freedom of an imaginative tour, essentially a destabilizing experience. The proposition of a moral posture, and its immediate demolition ('You exaggerate! You do exaggerate! You know you do'), has the effect of loosening ideology, implying the absence of objective truths, and forcing the audience to make its own decisions about the actions shown or described. What the audience is given, its reward for this dangerous exposure, is beauty (truth having been annexed by political or psychological theory). *The Last Supper* is beautiful in language and form (I am thinking particularly of the parable entitled 'The obscure origins of domesticity'), whilst being wholly un-ideological. The play is no longer a proposition about politics at all, though it is certainly about freedom. Rather it is a journey without maps and without clear instructions to the audience, which is sometimes pained by the absence of hidden orders ('Detest this character', 'See the manipulation here', etc.), especially when the character himself lacks stability (Ella in this play is both without words, then highly articulate, and Marya's contradictions are only superficially madness – they are in fact perfectly commensurate with frustrated dominance). In all my work after *Don't Exaggerate* the audience is unable to withdraw into the security of known moral postures. This alone serves to eliminate 'entertainment' from its experience, since entertainment is impossible without very firmly drawn demarcations.

Rabey. *Scenes from an Execution* dramatizes how 'artists have no power and great imagination. The state has no imagination and great power'. Do you think this relationship is essentially antagonistic, one describing the limitations of the other's reach and reference?

Barker. It seems to me impossible that the State and the artist should enjoy anything but a fleeting similarity of interest, usually in the aftermath of a revolution when the artist mistakenly believes his imagination will be licensed as part of the cultural rebirth of a new order. The rapid restitution of economic and social priorities and the assertion of the collective, or its mediators, over the individual interpretation of society, make this inevitably short-lived. States are mechanisms of discipline, and perpetually involved in re-writing and re-ordering experience, annexing it and abolishing it in the interests of proclaimed moral certitudes. The artist, as long as he is in profound union with his imagination, inevitably finds himself opposing ideological imperatives and exposed to censorship. This censorship will always take the form of 'protection' of sensibilities (the weak, women, virtue, the family, our past, etc.) no matter what the ostensible pretensions of the regime – a left regime has to protect 'class' and 'reason' as well as all the rest, and is likely to be more restrictive than certain inert reactionary ones. Women have to be protected against abuse, and the family against its perpetual, but never total, dismemberment. The State is a mass of fictions held together by superior power. I believe this has been the case as long as the State has existed. The problem is to judge which fictions are necessary ones.

Rabey. How might the compulsion of audiences to witness transgression, as depicted in Jacobean drama, and your own, be distinguished from voyeurism? Can the stage release, as well as depict, the unlived life?

Barker. All descriptions and propositions of and about life in drama entail the possibility of imitation. But my plays do not operate as models of behaviour, recommendations or exhortations. They are not pathways out of collective life or manuals of mayhem. They do not attempt to demonstrate wrong life or detail paths to self-knowledge. Every play is provisional, just as every statement must be provisional. I have nothing to teach anyone. In any case, the pain and despair experienced by my characters hardly invite imitation, though conversely, there is no tragic dénouement which reinforces the existing moral consensus. Rather the plays remove, plank by plank, the floor of existing moral opinion in order to plead other, unarticulated causes. The audience (if there is such a thing, and since I do not seek a solidarity here, I ought to talk of individuals) feels itself bereft (and frequently exhilarated as a consequence) of its usual critical or empathetic equipment, and even insecure in its laughter, which is the last refuge of uncertainty. But this disarray is not sterile. Since there is a distinct absence of moral convention, the transgressor is not punished, the audience is obliged to arrive at its own judgement, not of situations it knows, but of ones it does not. What occurs in my plays is only partly life as it is known, after all. Mostly, it is unknown life. The audience is stirred at a subconscious level by the sheer volume of imagined life which the actors present. This is not voyeuristic, since it is not a fetishism around an observed action which leaves the witness transfixed but still hermetically sealed in his own moral posture. The possibility that is unlocked in the relations between characters drags the idea of hidden life into the forefront of consciousness. It is an acutely painful, and a half-reluctant, experience, to which individuals frequently return.

Rabey. When surrounded by normative systems of predictions, connecting with further normative systems of predictions, rather than with lived experience, one is in danger of being enmeshed in a climate of accrued debilitation – to quote *Don't Exaggerate*, 'the liars operate in the imagination, too'. But the subversive power of the imagination, and its address to an unwontedly full sense of human integrity, might reside in its unpredictability. In discovering integrity in action, the individual invents freedom for himself or herself in a non-ideological way, and becomes answerable to nothing and no one for validation. How close is this to the spirit of enquiry at work in *The Possibilities* and to your sense of theatrical surprise in general? Do the subversive powers of both comedy and tragedy lie in their demonstrations of essential incongruity? Is the vital essence of theatre a power of dislocation?

Barker. The hidden purpose of much modern drama has been the exposure of wrong life. The play states more or less overtly 'beware not to live like this', or in an age of ideology, 'you must put an end to this'. Both comedy and the sorts of tragedies we variously encounter conspire in this missionary intention. And it would be absurd to pretend audiences do not hunger for this instruction as vehemently as writers long to provide it. It is theatre's old obeisance to certain governing conventions. When the play fails to provide instruction in wrong life, unease is created and frequently, a piqued resistance. In *The Possibilities* I persistently refuse the answer an audience anticipates from the predicated situation. There is an element of frustration in it, but what prevents the witnesses of the plays from becoming vociferous in their unwilling subjection to the wholly unpredictable nature of the pieces is the peculiar, simultaneous ecstasy of recognizing the appalling strain of being human. They are not led or instructed by the story. The onus of dealing with the pain is theirs. There is no right course, or wrong action in *Kiss My Hands* or *The Philosophical Lieutenant*. Nor is there a generalized protest at the way we are, or our unkindness to each other. The audience suffers this, but the pain is somehow positive. It can only be that out of the deepest exploration of pain, unmediated by ideology or morality, a certain strength is lent by performance. The power of these pieces in production reveals the meaninglessness of the notion of 'pessimism' in art. It is not pessimism at all, it is the excoriation of experience.

Rabey. I know you resist sentimental or intoxicating celebratory invocations of 'community' such as some would identify as the characteristic cohesive effect of the theatrical experience – the descent (or imposition?) of communality which Hilton and others worship in mystical terms. Rather, you've emphasized the individual reflection of the single audience member, concentrating and witnessing in the darkened stalls. But what then is his relationship to his fellow spectators, and to what extent is this salient to the theatrical experience?

Barker. Yes, I am against the solidarity of the audience. It is easily manipulated and frequently, albeit unconsciously, authoritarian. The best moments in theatre for me are those in which solitary movements can be discerned, in which a sense of contest can be registered between the stage and the disjointed audience. These solitary contests are of course determined by the fact of the existence of others, they would be harder to achieve in isolation. The tension created by an assumed collectivity of response, which then disintegrates, leaving individuals exposed to the effects of actions on the stage, is to me a valid condition of experiencing art. The audience has to sense its moments of division as well as its moments of unity, which I would not deny, though I wouldn't locate this unity in the usual places, perhaps. The unity should surprise as much as the disunity. Often this sense of isolation is affirmed by the light of the foyer, where the normal buzz of the consensus is replaced by a wariness to articulate what is still undigested. But I do not intend the individual to be without a guide. I come back to the actor, who by sheer bravery becomes the focus of hope and the source of security that cannot, in my work, be found in the usual forms of the message or the verisimilitude. In the actor's courage, the audience individual finds his own.

A conversation with Charles Lamb

Lamb. You're writing increasingly on theoretical matters about theatre in general and the social function of theatre. Have you felt it necessary to do this? Because it could be seen, perhaps, as a rather dangerous direction for a creative writer to take.

Barker. Anyone who has worked consistently at an art form for a number of years has a theory of creation and production. It is only a matter of articulating it that separates 'theoretical' artists from others. In my own case I undertook it as a work of self-defence. Unlike most ostensibly 'controversial' writers I had no critical support that was visible. Where it existed, chiefly among younger academics, and abroad, it couldn't express itself in the public domain. With the 'Fortynine asides' (p. 17) I recognized that the aphoristic was the most suitable for me, given the poetic nature of my writing style. But the theory changes, as the plays do in temperament and form. I have never thought it likely the style of my work could be dominated by a theoretical posture I had adopted, but rather the other way round. I am seeking to justify, in a post hoc way, what I arrived at imaginatively – that seems the only way an imaginative artist proceeds, blindly, wilfully, and chaotically, in the first instance, conceptually on reflection. But I was inevitably drawn towards questions of function and the social context of theatre. There was no theory of production which did not see theatre as essentially a critical medium. I was bound to collide with that.

Lamb. Two things occur to me: one is that there has been a tremendous dominance of theory in this country in post-war theatre, in theatre as studied in universities – I'm thinking particularly of Brechtian theory and the influence of Stanislavsky. This seems to centre on theatre being a form of communication which disseminates messages or truths to its audience. But the problem with your kind of theatre is that it doesn't do that. Derrida has said that the literary work should be 'insupportable', meaning not only that it should somehow challenge our tolerance but that it should resist analysis in terms of current theoretical positions – that it should not depend on or refer to theoretical 'positions' for validation, rather it should question theory. And in a sense it seems to me that what you're trying to do with your work involves a reversal of the normal assumptions; critics go to performances expecting to come away with something – theory, message or whatever; they do not expect to have their own assumptions challenged.

Barker. This challenge to existing critics and existing audiences is not a politics on my part, not a mischief, but springs – at the point of creation – from exhaustion with forms and assumptions, the obsession with clarity, for example, that I regarded rather early on as being a lethal ingredient in practice. After all, I never write from clarity, I have none, nor do I ever know the structure or narrative form, let alone the content, of any play I am writing. How could a theory of production that depended on 'clarity of meaning' and 'intention' have any relevance to me? Those who clamoured for meanings and messages were requiring the theatre to reiterate social propaganda within the framework of a governing social humanism, a compact of mutual celebration which had degenerated into massage. My first assumption became – a statement from bitter experience – that the audience and the stage are not united, rather that the theatre is a place of discomfort, and that its prevailing mood is one of anxiety. It occurred to me, almost as soon as I had emerged from an ostensible 'socialist' form of 'critical' writing (not that it had earned me any friends among 'socialist' 'critics') that – given the plethora of media information, social propaganda, collective affirmation, humanistic accord, that falls here like a drenching rain – theatre's only function now could be speculation, beyond the existing humanistic compact, in other words, for the theatre to become an illegal space. Instead of taking theatre into the street, as if it could speak automatically to all people, it should assert its privileged nature, its secret character, claiming privacy for the very reason that privacy in a populist culture is anathema and the subject of perpetual violation. In a sense, it should be hard to get at. Obviously this is the opposite pole from the national obsession with 'access'. But access is only control in another form.

[208]

Lamb. Brecht and Stanislavsky, and the notion of the play as having a 'ruling idea' seem very prevalent in the kind of director's theatre we have here. The theatre theory of the twentieth century pivots round the figure of the director – not the figure of the writer. And that shift is especially concerned with the exercising of a kind of control, the control of the performance.

Barker. That is true, but writers have conspired in this; since Brecht in particular, but it extends far back into the Enlightenment: also, they have conceived of themselves as civilizers. If you think your function is to civilize other human beings, you can't permit yourself the dangerous luxury of seeing the performance 'degenerating' into ambiguity, the actors playing contradiction, and so on. It is primarily a matter of disciplining the audience and the performers into a condition where they are able to 'receive' the dispensed wisdom of the text. In essence I believe the actor to be a symbol of mayhem, an unreliable reservoir of emotion, a licensed player of the illicit. Modern directorial practice has been to pin him to a rack of ideology – in the supreme interest of the collective, of course. He is diminished by this, and so is the theatre.

Lamb. I wanted to talk about the actor because the best response to your work has been largely from actors and I would have thought their response would come on a more immediate, experiential and instinctive level. Whereas the position at the moment is that your work is not acceptable to the major theatrical establishments, which are essentially directorial establishments.

Barker. Yes. I don't think it is possible to exaggerate the absolute seizure of the theatre environment at the moment. This seizure is the outcome of a peculiar collusion between liberal theatre directors and populist culture as a whole. The values of entertainment and the degeneracy of a critical theatre into a new sort of sentimentality have produced a theatre which is indistinguishable from other dramatic forms, but almost certainly inferior to them. It is my view that theatre has been good only when it disassociated itself from the governing ideology, that it made its business the experience of outlawed life – and I don't mean the fashion for criminality. The natural outlaws of society are artists, of course, and not criminals, who merely mirror the values of ruling systems. I'm referring to

[209]

tragedy, which is trespass. Directorial theatre distrusts tragedy. It gets out of hand, is irrational. Most directors are uneasy with irrational qualities on stage, it gives them a sense of redundancy.

Lamb. Regarding the business of performance then, do you feel that there is a need for a new approach? One of the things that interested me in studying your work, considering it from the point of view of performance, was that it did seem to question the established functions of director and actor and the way in which these might approach the work of rehearsal and finally the performance itself. One of the things that struck me was the actors' insistence on the openness they found in your texts; so that when they went out to perform there was a sense that they did not know what was going to happen next. Now that sounds like nonsense because of course the text is there but perhaps they did not know what the motivations behind the words were going to be, what the implications would be, in which particular direction the ambiguities were going to tend or how another actor was going to play a line which they would then have to respond to. That openness interested me. One actress in particular, I seem to recall, did a lot of work on her part, examining all the different possibilities of the different situations but she would approach a performance with a sense that those possibilities were all still open.

Barker. This sense of fluidity – some actors might regard it as insecurity – reflects the manner of the production of the text itself, which, as I said before, was written in that state of chaos which I regard as normal with regard to my own work and life in general. Do we possess 'intentions' with regard to one another which are not in permanent overthrow? Do we not depend on a high degree of resourcefulness in our dealings with one another, seizing, abandoning projects, opportunistic at one moment, craven the next? The ambiguities that lie within speeches in my plays, the fact that characters proffer themselves, withdraw, exercise a desire, and even pretend to a desire in order to witness its effects, mean that both actions and speeches are ambiguous even to the character himself. An argument might be ridden like a horse by a character until a better presents itself – if only because argument in my work is frequently spurious, and only emotion is trusted, emotion conjures the argument out of need. Thus an actor will find it hard to lay down a line on a character from any rational point of view, all he can approach at any given moment is the emotional demand generated by his character encountering another. This must change night by night, and no actor can ever play this work blindly, or soporifically, as they frequently do with texts which are cemented; it is also why members of the audience frequently return to watch again and again – partly to witness different aspects of the overwhelming density of it, but also to see performances in flux. This means the director's role is a different one. He cannot be the fountain of 'meaning', his autonomy is distinctly limited, and authority is widely distributed. His crucial function is to orchestrate. It is an aesthetic judgement that is called for here, a fineness of sensibility to the overall experience.

Lamb. One of the things that interested me in this connection is the business of bluff. It seems to me that quite a number of your characters in quite a number of plays are bluffers – they fake. And I feel that this is an important characteristic of a lot of performance. The ambiguity of a situation connects with this in the sense that you can have a character who plays a reaction which is – for want of a better word – 'genuine' or 'unpremeditated' – such as, for instance, pain – that can at a certain stage turn into performance when the character realizes the effect this is having on others and begins to exploit it. This is the kind of area where the actor actually has choices because at what point does the bluff begin and the spontaneity end? It struck me this was an opportunity for the actor to live the situation differently every time.

Barker. It is the reason why the work is violently unnaturalistic, for naturalism takes fixed character for granted. This acute self-awareness in characters is the absolute in tenderness, in thin skin. The word *bluff* implies a conscious manipulation, but this is not strictly true. The character is always governed by powerful desires, ones which are more or less permanently out of control, and therefore in crisis, he grasps, expediently, desperately, at whatever lies to hand, sometimes with yet further appalling consequences. Stucley, in *The Castle*, Charles in *Victory*, my Vanya in *Uncle Vanya*, nearly everyone in *Ego in Arcadia*, to an extent perform their own emotions and exploit the opportunities lent by their fascination. Stucley's long speech to his wife on his return is a tortuous series of attempts to

[211]

undermine her resistance to him, but they are not calculated so much as driven by need, a sort of brilliance born of panic. In this panic, a number of narratives are going on at the same time.

Lamb. Yes, that's a good example. You can actually have the opposite thing. Stucley performs his weakness – and he is performing, but he can also be seduced presumably by his own performance? And actually, although he sets out to control this whole thing from a strategic point of view, the performance can take him over and he can end up being taken back by it, becoming the victim of his own performance.

Barker. When the character expresses an intense emotion – released by the breakdown of stratagems or appeals – it flings open doors, opens vistas to new grounds of invention. The attack on the Bible and the Christian message by Stucley, for example, is primarily an expression of pain and loneliness, but hearing his own articulation of it provides him with a new resource. He attacks the Bible, he rejects it, then he retrieves it, annexes it, for his own purposes, by inventing the theology of Christ the Lover. The spontaneity of these emotional swoops forces him into new postures, so he does become both the victim of his emotions and also the shrewd exploiter of them. Characters therefore swing between control and loss of control. Naturalistic theatre is always bound by the possible, in effect, the already known. In Catastrophic Theatre, the impossible is drawn into proximity.

Lamb. Presumably this is where language is very important because the language carries the momentum of the drama and the characters, through using language, can be seduced by their own articulation. So there is a sense in which perhaps the words speak the character rather than vice versa. I think this is another area in which there is a problem with contemporary performance theory which teaches actions – the Brechtian idea of 'gestus' where one considers the action as a whole and the words are merely part of it. In considering the text, one looks at the line and decides what the action is, the motivation, and then speaks the words following up that particular action.

Barker. In such a theory, the words become of diminishing importance, they might even be incomprehensible, whereas I have argued that the power of language is crucial to the authority of theatre, but that it has to be continually reinvented: the dramatist must also be a poet, just as the actors must equip themselves to speak. The speech is specific to theatre, one of its highest principles and what most distinguishes it from film or television. In the speech the actor breaks the bonds of the real, disrupts the familiar, scattered syntax of naturalism, with its domestic associations, and draws the audience into a state of intoxication. It is the antithesis of critical realism, with its 'on the one hand . . . on the other' formulations, its commitment to objectification. And the speech does speak the character. Articulation in such torrents subverts reason, unbalances the complacent notion of stable character. In floods of temper or despair we say 'I did not know myself . . . '.

Lamb. Moving from the theory to the work that you are writing: it's changed very considerably over the course of your career – especially these last few years. But if I actually look right back through your drama, there do seem to be certain central issues and concerns which are remarkably consistent. In fact I was very surprised at the way certain situations which loom large in plays of the 1980s are there in embryo in plays of the early 1970s. How do you feel that the direction of your work has changed recently?

Barker. There are new themes, but also, as you suggest, themes which are entirely re-viewed. The idea of sacrifice for example, which could only be approached satirically in early plays, has taken on enormous significance in recent work. Smith is the first of these self-sacrificing figures, the first example of pure devotion that I have managed. Indeed, the whole of *Rome* is about the conflict between definitions of self and the abolition of selfhood. Then there are the servant figures who predominate in my more recent work, beginning with the servant in *Ten Dilemmas*, a man morally and intellectually superior to his master, but moved to terrible acts of service by pity, and the former tutor Dancer in my latest play *Hated Nightfall*, who converts a passion for revenge into a supreme self-immolation. Some of these investigations can be traced back to *The Possibilities*, particularly perhaps to the Groom in *Reasons for the Fall of Emperors*, whose infuriating self-abnegation is only slightly ridiculous.

Another theme which colours recent work, but which it now seems clear had earlier, cruder manifestations, is the idea of the insufficiency of the world, of the impossibility of discovering a place in it for those whose souls are, in a sense, too large for their environment, whose curiosity is too intense for the mundane necessities of social order but too desiring for solitude. This is very much the texture of *The Europeans* and of *Rome*, but you are right to say it appears embryonically in earlier plays, say, *The Castle*, where the emotional ambition of Skinner cannot discover an equivalent, or *Crimes in Hot Countries* where Erica is condemned to spiritual loneliness for daring to dream of her equal. This ill-fit with the world was solved in *The Europeans* only by a series of semi-barbaric acts of existential will, induced by Starhemberg, suffered by Katrin. The search for a reason not to commit suicide lies at the heart of my work, and what is distilled from that is a sense of melancholy. The most melancholic of my plays is perhaps *Golgo*, though *Ego in Arcadia* is profoundly melancholic. I don't mean depressing. Only a populist, entertainment-obsessed, comedy-obsessed culture confuses melancholy with depression.

Lamb. I remember you saying once that one of your major interests was character. You also said that you were interested in the point where the personal intersected with power and the political element, this latter coming to be seen especially in the shape of ideology. With this emphasis on the individual – and a lot of your characters are concerned to discover or follow their individuality – isn't this perhaps another kind of ideology? Where will becomes a thing solely in and for itself? I'm thinking in particular of the attitude expressed by, for instance, Stagg, the Home Secretary in *The Hang of the Gaol*, when he asserts the importance of 'clinging' – with all the negative connotations that word implies. Your political figures are often 'clingers' in the sense that they sacrifice everything to their will to power; and in this sense your political figures are, in their grotesqueness, perhaps your most conventionally 'realistic' characters. I suppose what I'm suggesting is that there is desire but when this desire meets with resistance it can be sustained by will and that at a certain point the initial desire evaporates and there remains only will.

Barker. The political figures might be divided into the active seekers for power, and those on whom power is pressed. If Stagg is the ultimate cynic of a discredited democratic system, with its honours and compromised loyalties, perhaps Skinner is at the opposite pole, one for whom political power is the ironic gift of resistance to authority. The former exists in absolute circularity. The latter is burdened with the moral dilemma of inventing a new system out of the ruins of the old, and the horror of it causes her to repudiate power itself. It is only when she perceives – in a spasm of pure feeling – her chance to indulge her appetite for revenge that she picks up the keys again. These are different varieties of will, one sterile, one passionate. You could include Toplis, Park, Lear, Livia, Ridler among the willed, driven figures who are both made and ultimately broken by their collision with power. There is nothing remotely ideological about these, if ideology means, as it must do, system, structure, law and inhibition. They are transgressive, morally innovative, insisting on a personal identity which the collective seeks to eliminate. This reaches an apotheosis in *Ten Dilemmas*, where impotence is reclaimed as a form of opposition, and punished. This is not a case of will outlasting desire – pure negativity. The self denies social manipulation, even if self is partially – and I would insist only partially – socially produced.

Lamb. This obviously links with another aspect of your thinking which is concerned with the feeling of being menaced by increasing social authoritarianism. I recall you once saying that desire would possibly be made illegal. How real would you say this danger is?

Barker. The political and social project of the twentieth century has been the elimination of pain, the elimination of conflict, the prolongation of life. The corollary of this is the promotion of happiness. Apart from regimentation, which has been tried, the best means to achieve these ends is to create a barrage of propaganda about harmony, and this requires definitions. Profound moments of desire are disruptive, because by nature they do not relate to given norms, they defy the definitions arrived at by opinion-makers, whether it be intellectuals or Welfare State managers, media bosses, or vocal minorities. The increasing level of social propaganda, disguising itself as news and information services, entertainment and the various sham manifestations of 'participation', eventually must locate its enemies, it cannot define harmony if its opposite isn't visible. We have experienced some of this in the identification and paranoia over 'abuses', which has clear undertones of the medieval, the witch-hunt. The resource one possesses to oppose legalized happiness is imagination, of course, but we observe that in the theatre – to take one example – it is distinctly subordinated to social realism, now an oppressive form, as I have said elsewhere.

Lamb. One of the things that strikes me is the quantity of common ground you share with the classical Greek tragedians where one finds the opposition of collectivity and individualism formalized in the division between tragic protagonists and the choruses: the former demonstrating hubris by overstepping the bounds, the latter tending to present conventional social wisdom. You have attempted to assert the value of tragedy in a culture which is resolutely bent on endorsing comedy as being both 'healthy' and moral. Though what comedy does more than anything else – as Bergson points out – is reinforce collective values and attitudes.

Barker. I identified some time ago the pernicious effect of the comedy industry on moral autonomy here – it is one of the oppressive social characteristics that appears like a plague in *The Last Supper*, and, as you know, I have regarded political and social satire as the essence of redundancy.

Lamb. Another aspect of this is that you seem to share the Greek suspicion of the idea of happiness. This mistrust is a constant theme in the classical tragedies – 'Call no one happy until he is dead'. I think most people today would find this obsessive or morbid. Perhaps the Greeks felt that there was something more valuable than happiness – beyond happiness, which they saw as illusory.

Barker. It is the social endorsement of happiness – its politicization – that renders it more oppressive as a principle of existence even than when it was first institutionalized by the utilitarians. It has become a 'right', along with numberless other 'rights' that a populist State vomits from its cornucopia. Because the Greeks understood the pleasures hidden in the spectacle of pain, as well as its place in life, its supreme irrationality, even its comedy, they did not resist it in the way we do, even though it horrified them. They saw the malice in things. We have never really come to terms with the Christian god, because he has repudiated malice, it is not part of his will, despite the terrible fate of Job. Inevitably, the liberal humanist State dare not contemplate it either, actions of ill-will can only be the product of social malformation, psychological disturbance, and so on. Malice was a characteristic of the Greek gods, so that ill-fortune was not greeted with the nauseating incomprehension that afflicts us, the rage at the 'unfairness of things'. Also, they knew as well as we do that the acquisition of an object, or a person, delivers rather little satisfaction. The heroic consists in reaching beyond gratification, in rendering gratification irrelevant. Thus the idea of being happy does not concern Draper in *Ten Dilemmas* – it is not part of his consciousness any more. That he is bound to a woman with whom he cannot experience conventional 'fulfilment' is a source of fascination, and fascination is the highest state a character can experience in my work – an abolition of ends, absolute desire.

Lamb. You have characters who transgress and who break conventions and taboos in ways such as we've been discussing but there are always consequences to these actions. One of these seems to be that the character comes to an increasing solitude; they are progressively isolated.

Barker. Not inevitably, though solitude is a state I cannot say I find appalling or contemptible. It would be a most unimaginative culture that could not see the virtues of solitude, or the reasons why one might opt to exclude oneself from society. Men and women have chosen it for centuries. It is true that the relentless pursuit of knowledge can lead to nothing else – it's the fate of Savage in *The Bite of the Night*, and of Park in *Rome* – Park is physically deprived of the means of communication anyway. It arrives to some as a consequence of their supreme powers of resistance – they become idols: who in *The Castle* can discover the means of communicating with Skinner, for example? And in *Victory* it is an irony that Bradshaw spends the remainder of her life with an enemy who has also lost the power of speech . . . though there is a physical intimacy there. This isolation is a testament to their heroic status. Some are able to suspend it – Galactia, in *Scenes from an Execution*, is prepared to submerge it in a dubious form of celebrity, Lear in *Seven Lears* is prepared to play chess with a cheat for his whole life in order to engage at some level with another human being, but it is primarily the erotic that provides the sole recourse . . . it is the erotic that enables Starhemberg and Katrin to overcome the blandishments of the liberal State in *The Europeans*, and the erotic subverts Ridler's missionary zeal in *A Hard Heart*. At a certain point, however, there is a transition, a triumph, where solitude is resolved into a moment of universality. I am thinking of the sacrifice that Dancer makes in *Hated Nightfall*, when he expresses desire in a form which precludes the erotic. He draws catastrophe upon himself, and upon the family he has been ordered to execute, as a gesture of spiritual independence: more than a gesture, it is a rebuke to a world in which both the reactionary *and* the revolutionary are decadent, intolerable.

Lamb. Is this what happens with Draper in *Ten Dilemmas*? Because he ends up in a position where he's more or less forcing the others to kill him but he himself pre-empts that by taking his own life. In that situation there were other choices available to him – he could have bluffed, or pleaded. So that would be an example of someone going beyond isolation into sacrifice . . . ?

Barker. *Ten Dilemmas* is a play about rebellion, in its most extreme form, ultimate rebellion. It is a rebellion against nature, against sex and against procreation. Death is inevitable, and the collective – in this case the family of Draper – are prepared to murder him in order to break the fascination that exists between the fecund woman (Becker) and the impotent man (Draper). Draper's self-sacrifice might be seen, therefore, as peculiarly 'responsible . . .': Becker can do nothing but resort to another man, which she does in the last scene. But Draper's suicide is simultaneously the sacrifice required by the collective in full cry against a dissenter, and the act of a disdainful aristocrat who never for a moment doubts his power even if he suffers shattering despair. I cannot pretend to fully understand *Ten Dilemmas* yet . . . perhaps I never shall. In many ways *Hated Nightfall* is clearer to me . . . Dancer's lucidity, the defiance with which he sacrifices himself for a family who are not worthy of his sacrifice, is a perfect contradiction.

Lamb. We've talked about how you frequently present characters who assert their own individuality and are prepared to take this to excess, but you also show characters who do the opposite, who attempt to resign their individuality in servitude. Presumably you would not value this tactic of resignation of the will as highly as its assertion. Is it not as valid?

Barker. The idea of 'excessive' individuality is interesting. It suggests there is so much possible play in a personality that is submerged in the interests of order, discipline, political and social convenience, and if this is the case, then the theatre – as ever – poses the opposite, the unfettered, demonstrative ego. There are few victims in my plays – even the most resolutely punished of them all, Helen of Troy in *The Bite of the Night*, who is made the scapegoat for every failed system, turns her ordeal into a resource; her maimed body becomes an increasingly powerful talisman the less there is that remains of it. Armless and legless she remains an erotic fetish for succeeding generations. Katrin repudiates the idea of the 'victim' in *The Europeans* by thrusting her condition into the public gaze, an unrepentant hater. The victims of State power in *Victory*, Ball and Scrope, reverse roles: Ball becomes a silent, innocuous pet on a rope, while Scrope screams slogans at his tormentors. In a few cases, power becomes itself a tedium, and 'personality' a thing which, painstakingly made, loses its glitter. I am thinking of Toplis in *Crimes in Hot Countries*, Lear in *Seven Lears*, exhausted by enquiry, and the most potent example, Lvov in *The Last Supper*, a charisma at the end of its tether. Lvov has a household of 'servants', all of whom have renounced or try to renounce their egos in the interests of service to another. It is not until *Ten Dilemmas* that I dared to imagine the individual who yielded up his independence entirely to others, as opposed to the many characters who swing between submission and rebellion, as Lvov's disciples do. The servant in *Ten Dilemmas* is recognized by all around him as a man morally superior, intellectually superior, to those he has chosen to serve, who are themselves conventionally immoral. He does this from a profound sense of pity – not the lifeless pity we approve of socially, but a passionate love for two people engaged in a struggle *à outrance* with a mundane world.

Lamb. With your play *Uncle Vanya* it seems that you wanted to confront an aspect of English theatre which is reflected particularly in the popularity of Chekhov's plays. This is a kind of aestheticizing and celebration of hopelessness and apathy.

Barker. Works of art undergo changes of meanings from age to age, decade to decade. What I confronted in re-writing *Uncle Vanya* was the contemporary condition of the work. Chekhov may have thought his plays were comedies, but inevitably they have been annexed for other purposes, principally the endorsement of moral and sexual failure. The materialist argument that Chekhov was describing the decline of a particular class in the climate of gathering revolution may lend this moral weakness a certain documentary authority, but from the point of view of a living theatre, the effect has been to provide English audiences with an alibi for denying the speculative or the tragic. Chekhov, who seems to have hated the episode with the gun in *Uncle Vanya*, was so embarrassed by human action on the stage, as opposed to endless inaction, that he regarded this moment as melodramatic, shameful. I took this as my starting point for an unfolding series of incidents that obliged Vanya to reach for characteristics in himself that he could not normally expose, in other words, to lend him will. This castrated man is restored to his sexual powers and seduces Helena. Astrov, a fashionable ecologist, but still someone who cannot complete a desire, is murdered. The characters revolt against inertia.

Lamb. It's interesting that the shipwrecked Chekhov takes refuge in the room. In the sphere of theatre practice Chekhov is a very important figure – with regard to the development of Stanislavskian acting techniques. The 'system' could have been written to complement Chekhov's artistic vision – one of the striking characteristics of which is that there is no significant interaction. The plays dramatize the impossibility or worthlessness of this – as you say, it's a condition of negativity. So you have characters who are ceaselessly yearning towards each other but the play shows this to be hopeless and the only 'answer' is 'work'. The 'system' condones this vision by its emphasis on the primacy of the 'character', 'emotion' arising from the character's interior which serves to create an impression of the *role* as a precious but sealed balloon of subjectivity. Stanislavsky's 'system', like Chekhov, ignores the possibility of significant emotion being generated in and by the interaction of self with the other.

Barker. Yes, you have identified the crucial difference between my theatre and Chekhov's and between the Stanislavskian mode – with its domination of contemporary theatre practice – and what is required for my own practice. There is no carbonized stability of character in my theatre, no one is immune from the effects of others – on the contrary, the need to influence, subvert, annexe, seduce others is the very definition of existence. The consequence of this perpetual emotional imperialism or craving – it is a matter of judgement – is that action is the permanent state of affairs, that change is relentless, that the obligations of choice or denial cannot be evaded, and that selves are in constant play, every character has the potential for its own opposite. I have said often that the audience is – on an individual basis – given authority and autonomy by this sort of theatre, it is not trapped within the existent, not reminded, confirmed in its powerlessness. This dark, enclosed space, detached from the world, is a laboratory of human possibility. It has religious connotations, but whereas religion affirms disciplines, restrictions, theatre explodes them.

Lamb. A number of your plays – particularly recent ones – have contained clerics. And in *Rome* the central focus of the play is strongly ecclesiastical, involving not only individual characters but also the question of cultural identity as to exactly what 'Rome' is.

Barker. I think one has to examine the possibility that faith is one kind of freedom. We discussed the idea of servitude. What Smith performs in *Rome* is the absolute in priestly self-abnegation. She endures as literally as possible the ordeal of the man who has, stage by stage, become a god, just as God in this play manifests a terrible longing to be a man. Park, the immaculate Pope, is better at being God than God himself is, which is why he is condemned to suffer so inordinately. The reason Park has such authority is that he represents something superior to God – culture, 'Rome', the accretion of human artistic and social practice, which is in the end located in a fragment of a tea-cup. Smith's adoration of Park is inspired principally by his sexual pathos, but transferred to a set of values associated with 'Rome', few of which are ever identified: but that isn't important. What matters is her invention of an identity when social identity (the culture) is overwhelmed.

Lamb. The play is subtitled 'On being divine'. I'm interested in what your conception of the divine might be. Initially Benz is divine but clearly feels the need to engage with the human. He becomes engaged in a seductive deal with Beatrice which seems to propel him towards the human while she, on the contrary, overcomes what might be called her humanity – I'm thinking of her response to Benz's killing of their child. She says: 'There is the fact and the emotion. They come apart and in the gap's divinity.'

Barker. What is divine cannot be human, and what is human cannot be divine, therefore divinity is inhuman. We mean this even when we talk casually of 'divine beauty' meaning such exquisite beauty it is barely comprehensible, but there is a corollary to this, which is its moral detachment from human values. We know the Greek gods were without conscience, that the Old Testament God was jealous and vindictive, we even know that Jesus ran out of patience with the sick and tried to avoid them. We are frustrated by our own consciences and put limits to them all the time. This perpetual pull between the moment of authentic pity, which is rare, the trough of socialized pity, which is gesture, insincerity, public obeisance, and the violent repudiation of one's relations with others, which is a divine moment of moral autonomy, and of course, obscene if it were to become systematized, is the substance of the theology of *Rome*.

Afterword*

Do we have the theatre we want? Do we have the audience we want?

What is the meaning of 'we' in those two questions?

By what rights do 'we' 'want' anything? On whose terms? In whose interests?

The definitions inherent in these questions would be re-examined and reassessed constantly as part of the pulse of a vital culture. But it is hard to find any current debate of culture which carries through to ideas being tested in practical action, and even then the appeal and value of art – particularly drama, 'The Public Art' – tend to be defined and dominated by reference to an image of 'The Public', a monolithic restriction and distortion of possibilities, evoking characteristics such as habitual expectations and limited abilities in confronting depth, range, effect, change. Those who work in the theatre without conscious cynicism often feel constricted, compromised, even insulted, by having to diminish their engagement of efforts for this Procrustean spectre of 'The Public'. Some audiences and potential audiences do too, as theatre workers and audience members must have some human traits in common, surely?

Why? On whose terms? In whose interests?

Because drama is The Public Art it is usually implicitly interpreted as The Art of Solidarity. But – leapfrogging usual, implicit interpretations – what if a theatre located its aesthetic in addressing what lay beyond solidarity? Not everything that is 'public' can be identified as 'an act of solidarity' except by the most strenuous ideologue. 'What we have in common' is often invoked as our greatest sense of hope. The differences between us might be sources of hope, discovery and creativity also.

Theorists of drama, including Artaud and Brecht alike, make much of the submergence of the individual sensibility and ego into

---

* Originally published as the Introduction to the first edition of this book (John Calder, 1989).

[223]

a salutary corrective and/or relief provided by being united in a communal charge of feeling/thinking, the deliverance up of self to the reviving rush of instinctive entrancement or to the instruction of the greater yet humbler (because apparently anonymous) collective and its historical will. Such rhetoric of drama resembles that of sexual mystics who view the orgasm as a release from self rather than as a moment of profound self-consciousness. There is also a common implicit prescription of the sacrifice of the right to self-determination in the drama which 'takes you out of yourself' only to return you to the same essential shape, except more amused/enlivened/politically correct by virtue of this temporary release from the troubling complexity of individuality.

Howard Barker's drama centres on rupture, both external and internal, and the licensing of thought and feeling, instinctive expressions of human potential amidst its ubiquitous, often self-willed, restrictions. The writings collected in this volume are speculations towards a theatre in which audience members might be neither dismayed at, nor fearful of, the public expression or illumination of discrepancies between their reactions and those of their fellow audience members – and, indeed, discrepancies between their own reactions and their sense of what is commonly, socially right as a response, even perhaps what is right as their specific individual response. In this way, the theatre becomes a site of individual discovery, demonstrating the self's capacities for surprising moments of both intransigence and realignment. The unfamiliar permission of response, and the cowed, reflexively unified response it often provokes, is illustrated by this quotation from Barker's 1987 play *The Europeans*, where the Emperor addresses his courtiers:

> Sometimes you will want to laugh. And you will feel, no, I must not laugh. Sometimes you will suffer the embarrassment of one who feels exposed to an obnoxious privacy. You will feel, he should never have shown me that. And sometimes you will experience the terrible nausea that accompanies an idiocy performed by one for whom you felt respect. As if the world had lost its balance. I can only tell you, all these feelings I permit. So laugh when the urge seizes you, and then, be ashamed of the laugh. The Emperor only acts the insecurity of all order. Do you accept the truth of that?
> (*They shift uncomfortably.*)
> No one understands! Nihil comprehensa!

Indeed, audience individuals at a Barker play might find themselves capable of responses which are surprisingly shameless, as well as surprisingly shameful. Later in the same play, the Emperor proclaims the disturbing *aperçu* : 'No moment of unity is ever true!' (He is, of course, profoundly untrustworthy. So are all the voices surrounding him.) Alexander Leggatt identifies 'A fragmented world in which values are uncertain and the individual has to construct artificially a sense of his own identity – these are some of the basic conditions of Shakespearean tragedy'.[1] They are also basic conditions of Barker's catastrophism, which directly addresses the separateness of self in the breakdown of consensus. Barker has not characterized this separateness as necessarily to be feared, in defiance of populist sentiment of various hues and of attempts to ignore the breakdown of shared values and assumptions (as Jim Hiley has indicated, 'Liberal pundits don't like to be reminded of the collapse of the liberal consensus').[2]

Julian Hilton has implored of drama, 'If formal innovation is to succeed, it will have to break with the classical architecture of beginning, middle and end, as advocated by Aristotle, but also with the episodic theatre of the Brechtian kind. It must permit the possibility of moral and political meaning, but not depend on, or be circumscribed by, any single ideology'.[3] The rationalism – or more precisely pseudo-rationalism – so ingrained in twentieth-century British drama has impeded this innovation, remaining self-delightedly hypnotized by what Dragan Klaić has identified as 'the argumentative surface of rhetorics of conviction',[4] rather than being doubly disruptive of convention both in its address to unconscious and subconscious human drives and in its relationship between form and content (where form *becomes* content in experiential terms) – these are uncomfortable, because unfamiliar, directions for a drama striving beyond the dominant situation of the artist – self-consciously 'political' or not – and the audience seduced into pandering to expectations they have of each other, by way of the usual, implicit interpretations of The Public Art.

Barker's ambition to strive beyond past or present relationships between theatre and audience has led him to articulate and develop his own theories of how innovation might indeed occur, setting new terms for drama criticism and exposing the ludic regressions in the terms of the criticism currently written about him and others, with a view to advancing the argument; this collection aims to provide a concentrated focus and instrument of leverage to this effect.

In contrast to the confirmatory celebrations and deterministic didacticism which dominate and atrophy contemporary theatre,

Barker has rejected the reducible 'message' and, increasingly, the linear narrative, in favour of cumulative effects, variations on themes and contradictory experiences which rupture familiarities and conventional pieties to permit the release and range of the imagination. Incongruities, shifting identities, unpredictable events, with the disturbing power of a newly-forged myth, infused with the power of dream or nightmare – phenomena which are 'held together by connections which are emotionally powerful but logically inconsistent. Like life'[5] – or perhaps more like it than the omniscient air of pseudo-rationalist theatre, and with deeper and more persistent resonance. These are means by which form might, indeed, *become* content in experiential terms.

Barker's increasingly complex sense of character locates opposites which exist within each figure, so that there is no such thing as a stable character – any more than a stable audience, by implication; and Barker insists on exposing these contradictions, whatever confusion of conventional expectations (such as 'identifiable authorial viewpoint' or 'identifiable single message') results. His protagonists push their selves as far as they will go, no matter what the opposition or the awful discoveries entailed; his audiences are offered the chance to participate in and extend the discoveries depicted.

The subtitle to Barker's 1986 play *The Bite of the Night* – 'An education' – is a particularly felicitous choice, were one to interpret the process of education, not as systematic instruction or indoctrination, but rather as the challenge and development of intellectual, emotional and moral faculties: generating active thought in audience individuals rather than prescribing what they should think. This interpretative distinction between objectives is crucial in the evaluation of art and education alike. If only in this sole respect, one might make a connection between Barker's drama and Theatre-in-Education, another mode of drama intrinsically committed to the right of each audience member to work through and take away something different from the event, working through a method that is 'essentially heuristic', raising questions in the minds of its audience members that 'encourage them to reach for a change in their understanding', emphasizing 'redefinition rather than celebration'.[6] Elliot Eisner's distinction between educational objectives is salient here: 'instructional' objectives 'specify skills and information to be learnt'; 'expresive' objectives identify a situation in which audience members 'are to work, a task in which they are to engage: but

[226]

it does not specify what they are to learn . . . An expressive objective provides [both actor and audience member with] an invitation to explore, defer or focus on, issues that are of peculiar interest or import . . . An expressive objective is evocative rather than prescriptive.'[7]

Numerous Barker characters lecture, expound and digress, challenging the audience to listen and follow. The protagonists of the monologues *Don't Exaggerate* and *Gary Upright* are the starkest illustrations of this, but it is also significant that Savage in *The Bite of the Night* is a professional lecturer whose activity has been legitimized personally and dramatically by his one remaining student Hogbin, one of Barker's equally numerous pupil or acolyte figures, who frequently voice probable audience unease or incomprehension at the teaching that is afforded.[8] For all the unequal power, both need and want the other as well as resisting them, testifying to Barker's recurrent interest in the dynamics of mutual challenge, and the paradoxical processes involved in forcing another into a position of autonomy, instilling a hunger which might oblige them to become their own invention: a theme analogous to Barker's own dramatic practice. Also, renegades like Gary Upright, Sordido in *Women Beware Women* and Starhemberg in *The Europeans* challenge by maintaining that others are imprisoned in mind-forged manacles to some extent of their own choice and making; and if attempting to engineer their self-release involves the renegades taking human icons like Bianca and Katrin to the edge of madness or destruction, then they appear prepared to do so, attacking individual happiness or gratification at its juncture with social equilibrium, indicating a painful, terrifying freedom which might lie beyond conciliation. These renegades take it upon themselves to involve others in agonizing confrontations with the bars of their figurative prisons; but it is the prisoner who has to choose to walk out through the ruptured door, and to embark upon their own programme of harrowing self-determination.

My suggestion of affinities between expressive educational objectives and Barker's theatre is not negated by his statement 'I have nothing to teach anyone'; in fact, he provides a startling correlation of patronizing, placatory attitudes in the assertion 'We are in fear of our own audience, as a poor teacher is afraid of the class' ('Honouring the audience') and refines the terms of the encounter: 'Rather the plays invoke moral crises which deprive the audience of its usual judgemental opinion' ('Dialogue'). But beyond disruption, the plays also encourage the audience to reach for change, however difficult, in their understanding. This encouragement is generated by witnessing 'the doing of the undoable' – a challenge which occurs on two levels: firstly, on the level of witnessing Barker's dramatic characters undergo or submit to changes which defy our expectations or imaginings of what might be possible or conceivable for them to incorporate – and yet witnessing that incorporation occur, not only convincingly but compulsively; and secondly, on the level of witnessing Barker's actors undergo or submit to changes, in the course of representing these characters, which defy our expectations or imaginings of what might be possible for them or any actor to incorporate – and yet witnessing that incorporation occur, not only convincingly but compulsively. The sceptic might dismiss the occurrence of the first phenomenon as the barren fantasy of a romantic imagination, were the incontrovertible occurrence of the second not capable of achieving breakthrough, by which the occurrence of the first might be sensed as analogously, imaginatively possible. No wonder that some of Barker's most loyal and successful supporters and promoters have been actors; few dramatists issue such challenges, requiring such demonstrations of the paradoxical triumph of their craft, exploding and regenerating the configurations which, at any given moment, constitute 'human potential'.

The actor and director Ian McDiarmid, who has had a long and close association with Barker's work, asserts:

> So many actors, by the time they are asked to play the great parts, are encased in such self-protecting armour that they are no longer equipped to play them. They lack the breath and the breadth. Instead of embracing the part, they find a way of keeping it at arm's length, of avoiding playing it. It is wrong for an actor to contain a part, he must open himself to all the facets the part contains. The central dynamic is to be found in the collision of the contradictions.

McDiarmid's comments on playing Shakespeare are also pertinent to playing Barker:

> Naturalistic techniques are not appropriate . . . The plays aim for a distillation of life, not an imitation of it. Naturalism, or theatrical behaviourism, as it may more properly be labelled, is a formula, guaranteed to rob words of their value, to limit the actor's means of expression and deny those who people the plays their essential humanity and hence their

universality. The act of acting is itself the articulation of an intellectual and emotional response. Therein lies its vitality.[9]

Rather than as a minister of solidarity, McDiarmid regards the actor as an 'archetypal outsider' who 'disrupts harmony and confuses morality'.[10]

Similarly, so many audiences, instead of embracing play or performance, find a way of keeping it at arm's length, of avoiding engaging with it; similarly, so many directors, and critics. Thus, actors, audiences, directors and critics collude in a self-compounding spiral whereby intellect and emotion are continually displaced by trivializing witticisms. Bernard Shaw's reflection on his days as a theatre critic remains enragingly pertinent: 'When my moral sense revolted, as it often did to the very core, it was invariably at the nauseous compliances of the theatre with conventional virtue'.[11] Thus is bred a theatre of insecurity, which lionizes conventional values for the attempted reassurance of those confined to perpetuating them, in an attitude of willed myopia.

On the other hand, the event of theatre might be the surprising confluence of various parties searching for knowledge, in their own ways, on their own terms, and finding themselves empowered to make new imaginative discoveries. Brian Bates:

> Personal knowledge leads to power. But it is not a power to dominate and control others, which stems from personal insecurities. Rather, it is the power to direct one's own destiny in the face of pressures to lead a life defined by the well-rutted channels. While the supposed aims of scientific psychology are to 'predict and control human behaviour', the way of the actor aims at self-understanding, which may render the person *less* predictable and controllable by outside forces . . . The way of the actor adds nothing to our lives. Rather it *takes away* ; blocks, restrictions, fears, boundaries and conventional views of the self and experience.[12]

However, it is worth adding that this demolition of the habitual adds, at least, new challenge; demands a reach of want to surge into the vacuums created by the demolished self-restrictions, and thus the process of self-redefinition begins, on the shoulders, as it were, of the drama witnessed.

Barker has emerged, unique in his generation and country, as an aesthetic–existentialist theorist who dares to match the disturbing power of Wilde, Nietzsche and Sartre, and dares to develop both classical and revolutionary ambitions into speculations towards new

[229]

theatres, new cultures. Beyond even this, his drama and poetry work in an arena, and towards an aim, of his own making and constant remaking: specifically, the soundings of profound personal difference by a central series of images or initiatives; and the very exploration of change, the dynamic which rips people out of their former selves, more alive but raw and bleeding, and impels them into a journey through uncharted territory where things and persons are constantly on the verge of turning into their supposed opposites: one's act of courage and faith might strike another as a bolt of the most profoundly painful evil. These collected philosophical epigrams and essays are pursuits of enquiry, challenging the theatre to anticipate its own identity, discover its creativity in new terms which might oppose their very existence to habitual associations, presented circumstances and the constraint of imagination by imposed status: arguments for an as yet non-existent theatre, which would thrive on arguments *in* the theatre as a manifestation of vitality, a mortar of change, beyond fear or shame. Rather than be stifled into mute or laughing inertia by deference to the myth of The Public, which has displaced courage from the centre of most theatres (On whose terms? In whose interests?), participants in the theatre which Barker envisions might separately express or discover disunity which, when publicly emblazoned, becomes beautiful and terrible, excessive and frustrating, wounding and splendid. Here, contrary visions of purity are necessarily and permanently at war with each other, as are different levels of self-knowledge and hope. Here, polarizations fracture, stability dissolves, and love and ruthlessness co-exist in the same person, in the same action. Authority and profanity split open against each other, exposing, in each, both fears and anticipations of possibilities of regeneration.

Notes

1 *English Drama: Shakespeare to the Restoration, 1590–1660* (Longman, 1988), 59.
2 *The Listener*, 15 September 1988, 42.
3 *Performance* (Macmillan, 1987), 152.
4 Conference on Terrorism and Politics in Modern Drama, 4–10 September 1988, IUC Dubrovnik.
5 Brian Bates, *The Way of the Actor* (Century, 1986), 136–7.
6 Charmian C. Savill, 'Theatre-in-Education in Wales', *Planet* 67 (Feb.–Mar. 1988), 49–54.
7 Quoted by Tony Jackson in *Learning Through Theatre*, ed. Tony Jackson (Manchester University Press, 1980), 77.

8 Other examples in Barker's canon are Downchild and Stoat in *Downchild*, Gaukroger and Pool in *Pity in History*, Toplis and Music in *Crimes in Hot Countries*, Sordido and both The Ward and Leantio in *Women Beware Women*, Lvov and the disciples in *The Last Supper*.

9 'Shylock' in *Players of Shakespeare 2*, ed. Russell Jackson and Robert Smallwood (Cambridge University Press, 1988), 47.

10 *Ibid*, 54.

11 *Three Plays for Puritans* (Penguin, 1946), 13–14.

12 *Op. cit.*, 9, 202.

Appendix: other works by Howard Barker

Plays

Stripwell *and* Claw (1977)
Fair Slaughter (1978)
That Good Between Us *and* Credentials of a Sympathiser (1980)
The Love of a Good Man *and* All Bleeding (1981)
No End of Blame (1981)
The Hang of the Gaol (1982)
The Loud Boy's Life *and* Birth on a Hard Shoulder (1983)
Victory (1983)
Crimes in Hot Countries (1984)
The Power of the Dog (1985)
Scenes from an Execution *and* The Castle (1985)
A Passion in Six Days *and* Downchild (1985)
The Possibilities (1987)
The Bite of the Night (1988)
The Last Supper (1988)
Women Beware Women (1989)
The Europeans *and* Judith (1990)
Seven Lears *and* Golgo (1990)
Collected Plays, vol. 1 (1990)
Early Hours of a Reviled Man *and* A Hard Heart (1992)
Brutopia, Uncle Vanya, Ten Dilemmas in the Life of a God *and* Rome, *in* Collected Plays, vol. 2 (1993)
Ego in Arcadia
Hated Nightfall

Poetry

Don't Exaggerate (1985)
The Breath of the Crowd (1986)
Gary the Thief/Gary Upright (1987)
Lullabies for the Impatient (1988)

The Ascent of Monte Grappa (1991)

(all published by John Calder)

Opera

Terrible Mouth, music by Nigel Osborne (Universal Edition, 1992)